Harriet Martineau

Harriet Martineau (1802–76) was in many respects a daughter of the Enlightenment. Born into a manufacturing family of Unitarian commitment, Martineau received a good education for a woman of her day, which served her resolve to write about the social issues of the time. In this biography Martineau's life and work are examined in light of her contributions to social science, particularly political economy and sociology. She shared with many of her Victorian contemporaries a conviction that scientific knowledge was vital to social progress. An inveterate educator, Martineau wrote over seventy volumes and hundreds of articles and newspaper leaders. Her optimism and faith in the future were tempered by a concern about the "uncertainties of the age" – economic cycles, class revolutions, slavery, the subordination of women, neglect of children, religious conflicts and intransigence in politics. She was one of the most significant figures of her time. Her analyses and recommendations were taken seriously by Lord Chancellors and workers alike.

Susan Hoecker-Drysdale is an Associate Professor of Sociology at Concordia University in Montreal.

Berg Women's Series

Gertrude Bell	Susan Goodman
Mme de Stael	Renee Winegarten
Emily Dickinson	Donna Dickenson
Mme de Châtelet	Esther Ehrmann
Elizabeth Gaskell	Tessa Brodetsky
Emily Carr	Ruth Gowers
George Sand	Donna Dickenson
Simone de Beauvoir	Renee Winegarten
Elizabeth I	Susan Bassnett
Sigrid Undset	Mitzi Brunsdale
Simone Weil	J.P. Little
Margaret Fuller	David Watson
Willa Cather	Jamie Ambrose
Rosa Luxemburg	Richard Abraham
Sarah Bernhardt	Elaine Aston
Annette von Droste-Hülshoff	John Guthrie
Dorothy L. Sayers	Mitzi Brunsdale
Natalia Ginzburg	Alan Bullock
Else Lasker-Schüler	Ruth Schwertfeger

Harriet Martineau

First Woman Sociologist

Susan Hoecker-Drysdale

BERG
Oxford / New York
Distributed exclusively in the U.S. and Canada by
St. Martin's Press, New York

To The Memory of My Mother

Elizabeth Augusta Kaiser Hoecker (1902–1985)

Published in 1992 by
Berg Publishers, Inc.
Editorial offices:
165 Taber Avenue, Providence, RI 02906, U.S.A.
150 Cowley Road, Oxford OX4 1JJ, UK

© Susan Hoecker-Drysdale, 1992

British Library Cataloguing in Publication Data
Hoecker-Drysdale, Susan
   Harriet Martineau: First woman sociologist.
   I. Title
   301.092

      ISBN 0–85496–645–5

Library of Congress Cataloging-in-Publication Data
Hoecker-Drysdale, Susan.
      Harriet Martineau, first woman sociologist / by Susan Hoecker
   -Drysdale.
            p.   cm.   —   (Berg women's series)
      Includes bibliographical references (p.   ) and index.
      ISBN 0–85496–645–5
      1. Martineau, Harriet, 1802–1876.   2. Women sociologists—Great
   Britain—Biography.   3. Sociolgy—Great Britain—History—19th
   century.   I. Title,   II. Series.
   HM22. G8M344   1992
   301'. 092—dc20
   [B]   91–33223
                                                              CIP

Printed in Great Britain by
Billing & Sons Ltd, Worcester

Contents

Acknowledgments

The author wishes to acknowledge the support for this project provided by research grants from the Social Science and Humanities Research Council of Canada, and to thank Patrick Mates for his assistance.

The author would like to thank the following for permission to print or reproduce materials:

The National Portrait Gallery for the portraits of Martineau by George Richmond, R.A., and by Sir Richard Evans, and the photograph whose artist is unknown.

The Bodleian Library, Oxford, for the lithograph by Miss M. Gillies.

The estate of Cecil Woodham-Smith for the letter by her to Dr. Gillie.

Other photographs are in possession of the author or were taken by the author.

A.D. Martineau for use of documents of Harriet Martineau in his possession.

Richard Martineau and Mrs. John Martineau for use of the Reeve-Martineau letters and for hospitality and support during the research.

Dr. R.S. Speck for access to his collection of Martineau correspondence as well as the hospitality which he and his wife Ann generously provided during a research trip to San Francisco.

Professor R.K. Webb for his encouragement regarding this project.

Special thanks to Don Munro at the Institute of Historical Research, University of London; and to the Smiths who have always welcomed me at the Knoll.

The author wishes to acknowledge the assistance and cooperation of the staff at the following libraries and archives:

Library of Manchester College, Oxford
The University of Birmingham Library
The Bodleian Library
The Fawcett Library
Institute of Historical Research, University of London
London School of Economics Library
Dr. Williams Library
The British Library
Royal Commission on Historical Manuscripts
Central Library of the City of Birmingham
Cumbria Record Office
Norfolk Record Office
Vanier Library, Concordia University

Gratitude is extended to Dr. Marion Berghahn, Berg Publishers, for her patience in waiting for the manuscript and for her advice and support at each stage of the project. It was my pleasure to work with Pat Morrissey, copy-editor, whose suggestions, made with enthusiasm and sensitivity, surely improved the text, and with Ellen Maly, editor.

The author is indebted to many individuals who, through their expertise, encouragement and assistance in various ways, have helped to make this project a reality: Marianne G. Ainley, my friend and colleague, who read the manuscript in numerous versions, and provided scores of useful and important suggestions and utterly unfailing encouragement; Dana Hearne, with whom I have shared many exciting and valuable discussions about feminists in history and the challenges of writing about them; Katherine Waters, with whom I have enjoyed years of friendship and collegiality, Roslyn Belkin who gave me sisterly encouragement to get the project underway; Michael Hogben for his computer expertise and, with Margaret Simpson, friendship; James Hoecker, who shares my interest in British intellectual history and who, unlike Harriet's brother James, has always given unquestionned support; and Gerd Schroeter for his useful critique of the research proposal. Penny Pasdermajian has provided valuable assistance in the research and generous help wherever needed during the past five years. Roslyn Yearwood in the Department of Sociology, Concordia University, has shared the whole experience in good humor and looked after me in many ways. Robert Tittler, Leo Bissonnette, Wendy Knechtel, and Theresa Portugais, have helped in important ways to facilitate my work. Relatives and many friends who have shared somehow in this project, at least suffered through its interminable writing, will no doubt be relieved to see the end. I thank them for their support. I am most indebted to John Drysdale and David Drysdale, who have had to live with Harriet Martineau as well as a frenetic author. Their love, encouragement, support and understanding have made it all possible, worthwhile and meaningful.

Illustrations

Abbreviations

Abbreviations used in the text (for full reference, see Bibliography)

Auto.	*Autobiography*, 3 vols.
BS	*Biographical Sketches*
DN	*Daily News*
EL	*Eastern Life: Past and Present*
ER	*Edinburgh Review*
FC	*The Factory Controversy: A Warning Against Meddling Legislation*
HHH	*Health, Husbandry, and Handicraft*
HE	*Household Education*
HM	Harriet Martineau
LLMN	*Letters on the Laws of Man's Nature and Development*
LS	*Life in the Sickroom*
LWR	*London and Westminster Review*
MR	*Monthly Repository*
RWT	*Retrospect of Western Travel*, 3 vols.
SA	*Society in America*, 3 vols.
WR	*Westminster Review*

Introduction

This book is about the life and work of Harriet Martineau (1802–1876), English public educator, sociologist, historian, and journalist. Martineau has been seen generally as a fiction writer and popular educator. Although she wrote poetry, short stories, novelettes, and novels, her nonfiction, whose subject matter lies in economics, history, sociology, social psychology, and geography, constitutes the greater part of her published works. Indeed, her fiction as well as her nonfiction were written to educate her readers about such issues as slavery, colonialism, women's condition, middle-class marriage, community relations, the history of religion, industrialization and capitalism. The purpose of this intellectual biography, therefore, is to present Harriet Martineau as a significant figure in the tradition of British social science and of nineteenth-century sociological thought. Robert K. Webb stated in 1960 that Martineau had been preaching sociology for much of her life. In a 1973 essay Alice Rossi identified Martineau as the first woman sociologist. And in 1989 Michael Hill reminded us that Martineau's pioneering work in sociology in the 1830s went unrecognized. Sociology was not an established academic discipline then, and Martineau, however influential and well-known, was a woman in a patriarchal intellectual context.

Martineau's intellectual perspective and her self-consciousness as an analyst of her times placed her, very early in her writing career, in the arena of the moral or social sciences. Through her extensive reading and contacts with the leading intellectuals and public figures of the period, she became committed to the "moral sciences" because she believed that they would provide the new knowledge and understanding about the laws of human nature and human society which were required for social progress.

Harriet Martineau believed that progress and a more rational and just society would be ensured by the expansion of industrialization and capitalism, but that these necessitated an informed public who understood the principles of political economy, democratic government, dutiful individualism, and social co-operation. Martineau saw herself as a public educator. She popularized contemporary studies in economics, philosophy, and science and interpreted the major doctrines of her day. From her first publications at age 19 to her last major writings at 74, she took up a wide range of subjects and issues in a variety of genres, publishing over seventy volumes, dozens of periodical articles, and nearly 2,000 newspaper leaders and letters. A life occupied with writing was complemented by travels to America, the Middle East, Ireland, and Scotland. She also travelled "in armchair" to many other places and chronicled them so scrupulously as to fool many readers about her actual itinerary.

This presentation of Martineau's life, ideas, and contributions is a exploration of her sociological understanding of a world on the threshold of modernity. She embraced the social changes she saw and wished to share her enthusiasm. From her early days of authorship she searched for a systematic and inspiring doctrine which she could use to guide her generation through these transformations. This quest ultimately led her to French sociology. Her 1853 translation of the *Cours de Philosophie Positive* of Auguste Comte, the founder (with Henri de Saint-Simon) of French sociology, constituted a significant contribution to the dissemination of sociological positivism and appeared, however briefly, to be the answer to her search. That task was not an isolated achievement in Martineau's career, however. Her sociological proclivities had first appeared in her contributions to the *Monthly Repository* in the 1820s and developed further in the next decade in her tales on political economy, taxation, and the Poor Laws. It was, however, her investigation of American society which provided the first occasion for exercising her research skills "in the field." She produced, in addition to two three-volume studies of American society, the first methodological treatise in sociology, which contains insights of value even for today's researcher. Her sociological perspective expanded in later writings on the Middle East, Ireland, and India, in her history of England and her explorations in science and positivism.

Harriet Martineau was a feminist as well as a sociologist. Her concerns about the condition of women in society form an important part of her studies and of her interpretation of social progress. Martineau wrote about women writers and gave women

2

salient roles in her fiction to illustrate certain principles of social life. In her nonfiction she analyzed women and work, women and education, marriage and family life, women's dress, women, politics and the law, women and birth control, prostitution, women and the arts. Although excluded from university education and the resources which in the nineteenth century only men enjoyed, Martineau had a major impact on public opinion, politicians and government policy makers and her contemporaries interested in the social sciences.

Harriet Martineau was a daughter of the Enlightenment. She was committed to rationalism in several different respects. The emotional turmoil of her childhood created a need for order in daily living and a sense of distance, or detachment, from even her closest friends and relatives. Quite religious as a child, she was drawn to philosophy and science by her early twenties, when she began to publish in the *Monthly Repository*. Just as she recognized her love of writing and her ability to do it well, she also realized that she must develop a vocation which would provide economic independence and personal autonomy. She organized her daily routine around a schedule which allowed a minimum six-and-a-half to seven hours for writing. She wished to be dependent on no one – neither her family, a spouse, friends, neighbors, nor the government. In some respects she was judgmental, toward herself as well as others, determined in her assumption of a male role in the public world, and, some have claimed, repressed in her denial of the feminine dimensions of her life. But she was also a generous, warm, cosmopolitan, sociable, active, and enthusiastic citizen of the world, a woman who wished to be a part of the debates and events of her time, even if from her sickbed in Tynemouth or her writing desk in the quietude of the Lake District. We will try to show how her life reflects her vocation and her dedication to social progress. Her achievements, her influence, and her place in nineteenth-century society are unique and remarkable. No one before or since has played the very special role in history which was hers.

A word about the organization of the book. Martineau's life and work are treated concurrently in each chapter. The chapters are arranged in chronological and occasionally thematic order to show the evolution of her thought and the progression of her writings and their subject matter. In a few places it was necessary to consider together writings from slightly different time periods because of their thematic links. In the interest of brevity, much material, for example correspondence, had to be excluded.

This book is an introduction to the life and work of Harriet Martineau as a sociologist – a sociologist in practice rather than in title. It is therefore a book for those unacquainted with her rather than for the specialist, who nevertheless may find here a new perspective on Martineau. The author is currently completing a critical analysis of Martineau's sociological works.

Harriet Martineau died on this day 115 years ago. She left an influential legacy of writings addressed largely to the main social, political, and economic issues of her time. This book is an attempt to contribute to the recovery of the legacy of this remarkable woman's life.

Montreal
27 June 1991

WINTER

1 The Young Dissenter

Sapere aude! Dare to use your
own understanding! is thus the
motto of Enlightenment.
— Kant, "What is Enlightenment?" 1784

Harriet Martineau observed in her *Autobiography* that she was born in the winter of her life. The sixth of eight children born to Elizabeth and Thomas Martineau of Norwich, she entered the world on 12 June 1802.[1] The roots of this remarkable English family can be traced to Gaston Martineau, a young Huguenot surgeon from Bergerac, France, who emigrated to England in 1686 after the Revocation of the Edict of Nantes. Gaston subsequently married Marie Pierre de Dieppe, whose Huguenot family had also emigrated at that time; the couple settled in Norwich. Although medicine became the family profession, one great-grandson Thomas, Harriet's father, became a textile manufacturer in Norwich. This business afforded the family a comfortable existence until its failure in the bank and stock crises of 1825–26.

Norwich, with a population of approximately 60,000, was known in that era as the Athens of England, a cultured, sophisticated, and beautiful city, attractive to the middle classes and the progressive ranks of society. Its established connections with the Continent resulted in growing Flemish, Dutch, and French populations with their flourishing institutions. It was a favorite city for Huguenots, who numbered 8,200 in 1828. Political radicalism, including (later) Chartism, and general sympathy for continental political causes gave the town a singular reputation. Cultural life included an outstanding library, music festivals, and a sophisticated social life, in which Unitarians participated significantly. The important textile industries of Norwich, which helped to build a prosperous base in the eighteenth century, were threatened after the turn of the century by disruptions stemming from war, a decline in exports, and economic depressions (especially 1825–26), and the city changed markedly. The size of the working class enlarged, and an

7

increasing number of unemployed weavers and others generated strikes and strife which introduced young Harriet to class and class conflict (Webb 1960, 52–64).

Thomas Martineau, "a man of more tenderness and moral refinement than force of self-assertion" (Drummond 1902, 3:3), married Elizabeth Rankin, the eldest daughter of a Newcastle sugar-refiner. Descriptions of Elizabeth Rankin Martineau vary from "ordinary but talented" to "demanding and cold". Yet despite her own limited formal education, she insisted that all her sons and daughters be well educated, equipped to enter society and serve it well.[2] And, although Elizabeth Rankin was apparently uncomfortable about her inability to communicate in French with her husband's relatives and foreign visitors, she ensured that her children learned the mother tongue of the Martineaus.

From the beginning health problems marred Harriet's childhood. Either popular practice or an inability to nurse dictated that Mrs. Martineau hire a wet nurse for her sixth child. Because of the wet nurse's low milk supply, kept secret by the poor woman, Harriet nearly starved to death in the first weeks of her life. Her mother attributed her later illnesses and physical weakness to this deprivation. As an infant Harriet convalesced at the Carleton cottage of a Calvinist couple named Merton which, she reported later, made her "the absurdist little preacher of my years," emitting such maxims as "Never ky for tyfles" and "Dooty fust and pleasure afterwards" (*Auto.*, 1:12). Calvinism, at least the work ethic, left a lasting imprint on Harriet's character.

The liberal Protestant culture of the Martineau family, with its own ancestral experience of persecution, maintained a household atmosphere which emphasized toleration, intellectual development, and social responsibility. Thomas's business orientation no doubt contributed to the idea that material success and stability were also admirable goals. Most important was the Unitarian commitment, to a relatively higher degree than that found in other segments of society, to sex equality in education and personal development.

Nevertheless, within this particular family setting Harriet's childhood and youth were often difficult and at times discouraging. Years of stressful and demanding relations with her family, together with a series of early health problems and handicaps

8

produced a fearful, diffident young girl. Various relatives, particularly her mother, made her feel that she was ugly, or at best plain, and rather a nuisance because of her impaired hearing and oversensitivity.

Physical difficulties and anxieties about personal incapacities seemed to precipitate indelible fears and phobias, which were hidden from her family or, if known, were ridiculed.[3]

> I was as timid a child as ever was born; yet nobody knew or could know the extent of this timidity; for though abundantly open about everything else, I was as secret as the grave about this . . . Some of my worst fears in infancy were from lights and shadows. The lamplighter's torch on a winter's afternoon, as he ran along the street, used to cast a gleam, and the shadows of the window frames on the ceiling; and my blood ran cold at the sight, every day, even though I was on my father's knee or on the rug in the middle of the circle round the fire (*HE*, 90, 98).

Martineau described herself as "a poor mortal cursed with a beggarly nervous system." She could neither taste nor smell. Only once in her adult life, while eating leg of mutton, did she fully enjoy the sense of taste. The sensation was temporary; later that day the sense abandoned her again. She recalled that her sense of touch alone provided any pleasure of the senses. By the age of twelve Harriet developed a hearing problem; by fifteen it had become "very noticeable, very inconvenient, and excessively painful to myself" (*Auto.*, 1:72). Although in later life Harriet became famous for her ear trumpet, she did not use one until her late twenties because she feared ridicule, and with good reason. Her family not only derided her deafness but accused her of being stubborn, and even deliberately difficult.[4]

Elizabeth Martineau rarely showed affection to Harriet; instead she occasionally ridiculed her and, it seemed to Harriet, favored her brothers and sisters. These unsatisfactory family relationships combined with Harriet's sensitivities to create desperate cravings for heaven (even through suicide). She fantasized about angels coming to collect her as she sat in the Octagon Chapel at Norwich.

At the age of seven Harriet spent a summer at the home of her maternal grandparents in Newcastle. There she met fourteen-year-old Ann Turner, the daughter of a Unitarian minister, who became her first friend. Ann Turner helped to strengthen Harriet's religious convictions and to convince her that she need not be fearful and sad because others, including her mother, did care for her.

Although Harriet's family relationships became the subject of debate in posthumous biographies, early pages of her *Autobiography* reveal the pain and trauma of youth experienced by this shy, anxious, and sometimes quite desperate young girl. "I never did pass a day without crying" (*Auto.*, 1:43). She perceived herself as the strange one in the family, lacking the abilities, confidence, and social grace of her siblings. She detested the manipulation and injustice which she observed in people's treatment of others (particularly of her, and of household servants), and was especially sensitive to the vulnerability of the weak.

Confused and somewhat rebellious over both the family's treatment of her and the middle-class expectations imposed on her, the young Harriet found sanctuary in books and ideas. Her voracious reading and her early attraction to writing may be seen, in part, as compensation for the frustrations arising from her personal relationships. "I had no self-respect, and an unbounded need of approbation and affection" (*Auto.*, 1:19). Lack of confidence and a poor self-image, "I was always in a state of shame about something or other" (*Auto.*, 1:15), along with doubts about her acceptance in the family, produced a desire in Harriet to perfect some skill or talent with which she would gain their respect.

As a child Harriet showed great love and sympathy for others; she took great delight in her younger siblings and befriended a little girl who had had her leg amputated, but Harriet's mother ordered her to terminate that friendship on the excuse that Harriet would grow crooked under the constant weight of her friend on her arm. Harriet suffered "shame and regret" over having to tell the girl's mother that on her mother's orders she could no longer walk with her friend. Harriet also developed an early appreciation of, and respite in, nature as well as books. In her adult travels she paid particular attention to the varieties of flora, fauna and birds. Because she wanted to please, she learned to do everything as well as possible. Undoubtedly, her strong imagination helped her to survive, but it also cultivated the fears and phobias which contributed to her misery.

The Martineau girls were expected to develop traditional

skills in sewing and needlework. Harriet sewed all her own clothes, even her shoes, and for a short period prior to her writing success earned a living by the needle. In fact, Mrs. Martineau was convinced that sewing would provide the most suitable occupation for Harriet. Nevertheless, the Martineaus, following the Unitarian pattern, permitted the girls, as well as the boys, to have proper schooling. Harriet was first taught at home by her older siblings: French by Elizabeth, Latin by Thomas, and writing and arithmetic by Henry. These sessions were often painful, filled with sibling criticism and teasing.

Harriet studied the Bible and tried to clarify her religious beliefs, which centered on a beneficent God and the fear, not of punishment but, of sin and remorse for evil doings. "I did not care about being let off from penalty. I wanted to be at ease in conscience; and that could only be by growing good, whereas I hated and despised myself every day" (*Auto.*, 1:43). Harriet's religious convictions were supported by worship, music, and her study of *Pilgrim's Progress* and *Paradise Lost*, which she discovered at age seven:

> I was kept from chapel one Sunday afternoon by some ailment or other. When the house door closed behind the chapelgoers, I looked at the books on the table. The ugliest-looking of them was turned down open; and my turning it up was one of the leading incidents in my life. That plain clumsy, calf-bound volume was 'Paradise Lost;' and the common blueish paper, with its old-fashioned type, became as a scroll out of heaven to me . . . and my mental destiny was fixed for the next seven years . . . In a few months, I believe there was hardly a line in Paradise Lost that I could not have instantly turned to . . . I think this must have been my first experience of moral relief through intellectual resource (*Auto.*, 1:42–43).

In her search for religious truth, seven-year-old Harriet asked her brother Thomas "why we should be blamed or rewarded for our behaviour if God knows everything and decides our fate beforehand?" The answer left her unsatisfied, but even by the age of eight she had convinced herself of the power of patience and fortitude, very important to her in the years ahead.

At the age of nine Harriet attended a small school run by a Mr. Perry who, by converting from protestant trinitarianism to Unitarianism, had lost his pulpit and his former school.

Through Perry's instruction Harriet had her first happy learning experiences and developed her lifelong interest in books and writing. Armed with a knowledge of the classics, acquired at home, Harriet read and translated from Latin and French classics and enjoyed good instruction in composition and arithmetic. She later credited Perry's school with having launched her intellectual life. When it closed, other masters tutored the children at home in languages and music. The Martineaus encouraged their children to read history, biography and literature; Rachel and Harriet were also encouraged in needlework and music-copying. Harriet was attracted to Shakespeare, Bunyan, Milton, Malthus; to political economy, philosophy, and history. She devoured the novels and poetry of the Romantics: Austen, Wollstonecraft, Goethe, Wordsworth, and others. Her intellectual pursuits, however important, did not allay her anxieties. As a sensitive girl of fifteen, she was concerned about three problems: her bad handwriting, her deafness, and the state of her hair.

Although Elizabeth Martineau only sparingly displayed affection and warmth to her daughter, she seems to have given her support and encouragement at critical times. She tolerated her daughter's preference for the after-dinner reading of Shakespeare and newspapers rather than socializing with the family. This seemed to be a sympathetic recognition of Harriet's social discomforts on account of her poor hearing. After Harriet's early successes, her mother made helpful suggestions regarding the promotion of her publications and was presumably satisfied that her daughter was becoming economically secure. Harriet, for her part, paid respect to her mother and later provided her with a comfortable existence.

In the depth of adolescent worries a light appeared. Harriet was invited to Bristol (1818–19) to stay with her uncle and aunt Kentish who ran a boarding school for girls. Feeling inferior to the talents of her cousins, Harriet nevertheless became immersed in private study and cultivated her appreciation of natural beauty in the Bristol setting. But most important to her was her "dear Aunt Kentish," whose "free and full tenderness" during Harriet's fifteen months' stay satisfied her longing for human affection and countered her conviction that no one cared about her and her physical problems. The stay in Bristol was also highlighted by her friendship with the Unitarian minister Dr. Lant Carpenter.[5]

Her intellectual life flourished during this period. While schools provided a setting for her pursuit of learning, it was in private study that Harriet's intellectual growth accelerated. In addition to logic, rhetoric, history, and poetry, she extended her studies in Latin, Greek, and Italian. In fact, she developed a passion for translation and prided herself on producing translations from Tacitus and Petrarch. Later she translated from German and French with equal ease and enjoyment. She was more enthusiastic, however, about studying the Bible.

James Martineau, the seventh Martineau child, was born when Harriet was nearly three years old. From the beginning she mothered him and enjoyed his companionship, and he undoubtedly provided her with an emotional satisfaction missing in her relationships with the rest of the family. As they were growing up, she became emotionally and intellectually very close to him. "All who have ever known me are aware that the strongest passion I have ever entertained was in regard to my youngest brother, who has certainly filled the largest space in the life of my affections of any person whatever" (*Auto.*, 1:99). She was always lonely in his absence and heavily dependent on him for evaluation of her work and for important decisions.

James left for Manchester New College in York in the autumn of 1821. Anticipating Harriet's misery in his absence, he advised her to take up writing as a refuge. And so Harriet obediently initiated ("in my widowhood") a contact with the *Monthly Repository*, the important Unitarian periodical, submitting her first article, "Female Writers on Practical Divinity." Although she told no one of this important step, after it was published she reluctantly admitted to her eldest brother Thomas that the essay was hers. With a new tenderness and honesty toward her, he advised her to leave the sewing to others and devote herself to writing.

Although nervous and uncertain in everyday life, Harriet attacked intellectual tasks with courage and resolution (Wheatley 1957, 46). The spirit and determination which transformed difficulties and handicaps into accomplishments, respect, and independence also produced a determined personality and a style which often appeared judgmental and inflexible.

The Bible and contemporary religious writings, particularly those by her friend Dr. Lant Carpenter, inspired her to write *Devotional Exercises, consisting of reflection and prayers, for the use of young people* (1823) and *Addresses; with prayers and original hymns, for the use of families and schools* (1826). They were signed "By a lady." Martineau's first book-length tale, *Traditions of Palestine, or Times of the Saviour*, was published in 1829.

During the 1820s Harriet tried her hand at a number of genres, not always happily, though in general her success in publication was remarkably strong from the beginning. In her autobiography she recalls starting to write a "theological–metaphysical" novel, which was never published but which provided the occasion for establishing her philosophy of writing (*Auto.*, 1:121). With a typical sense of urgency she decided that it would not do to copy and rewrite her work, as she knew other authors, such as Maria Edgeworth, did. So, after copying only two of her earliest works, she concluded that "distinctness and precision must be lost if alterations were made in a different state of mind from that which suggested the first utterance." She followed Cobbett's advice – "to know first what you want to say and, then say it in the first words that occur to you" – and retained this approach throughout her life; her manuscripts are virtually unrevised (*Auto.*, 1:121–22).

> I have always used the same method in writing. I have always made sure of what I meant to say, and then written it down without care or anxiety, – glancing at it again only to see if any words were omitted or repeated, and not altering a single phrase in a whole work ... great mischief arises from the notion that botching in the second place will compensate for carelessness in the first ... I believe that such facility as I have enjoyed has been mainly owing to my unconscious preparatory discipline; and especially in the practice of translation from various languages (*Auto.*, 1:122–23).

Martineau showed an early interest in the ideas of Thomas Malthus and in political economy in general. These had developed out of her reading of the *Globe* newspaper and her geography text at Perry's school. She became fascinated with such matters as the national debt and government spending. Although the considerable popularity of Malthusian ideas nearly sickened her of his name before she was fifteen, as she told him amusingly some twenty years later, she was "all the while becoming a political economist without knowing it, and, at the same time, a sort of walking Concordance of Milton and Shakespeare" (*Auto.*, 1:71–72).

The impact of religious writings on the young Martineau was particularly strong and drew her interest to religious questions and social concerns. Her *Autobiography* reveals an early curiosity about the relation of the transcendent to the mundane, the religious to the social, the intuitive or inspirational to rational concerns and questions of life. She had an early interest in the implications of larger philosophical or theological questions about justice, goodness, truth, and love for the social existence of human beings. A passion for history and an intellectual openness also contributed to the development of this energetic young writer.

In the early nineteenth century, Unitarians, regarded as intellectual rationalists, contributed significantly to the culture of Britain (Holt 1938; Watts 1980). Among the important intellectual influences on Harriet were the poet (Mrs.) Anna Laetitia Barbauld and Dr. Lant Carpenter, who introduced Harriet Martineau to the philosophies of David Hartley and John Locke. Soon the impact of the social environment on human beings became an important part of Martineau's intellectual concerns. Joseph Priestley's book on Hartley provided her first scientific perspective on human behavior. She read the Scottish philosophers but did not at the time appreciate what they offered for an understanding of human society (*Auto.*, 1:106). The writings of the philosopher Dugald Stewart gave her a thorough introduction to the natural philosophy of Francis Bacon and to the basic paradigm of classical political economy, Stewart having been a major influence on David Ricardo.

These were the formative influences in the development of Martineau's scientific predispositions. She was impressed particularly with the then increasingly accepted doctrine of necessarianism: that natural and unchangeable laws in the universe determine the basis of human action and are beyond the control, if not the understanding, of human beings. According to this theory, no interference of divine or human will can change the consequent causal relations. In the early period of her life, however, this doctrine did not result in Harriet's rejection of religion, instead it clarified for her the function of prayer and the theological understanding offered by Unitarianism (*Auto.*, 1:114–16). Nevertheless, a rationalist perspective which was drawn to scientific positivism emerged in her thinking. Eventually, as she would later recount in her *Autobiography*, she rejected even, or perhaps particularly, liberal religion as anachronistic, "a mere fact of history," and found herself "a free rover on the broad, bright breezy common of the universe" (*Auto.*, 1:116). Far from rejecting the significance of religion in society, however, she defended Catholicism on many occasions and constantly advocated religious tolerance. In addition, her book *Eastern Life* (1848) illustrated her interest in the history of religions.

By her early thirties Harriet Martineau had evolved from a solitary duckling into a swan – the pleasant-looking young author of political economy tales, pursued by politicians, and lionized in London's literary circles. The personal difficulties of her childhood and youth, which had fueled her determination, now seemed to fade. The immediate success of her first political economy tale (which earned her thirty-one pounds) assured, at least temporarily, her solvency and considerably increased her self-esteem. It confirmed her aim to serve society through writing. And so it was upon the publication and immediate popularity in 1832 of *Life in the Wilds* (the first of twenty-five *Illustrations of Political Economy*) that the years of her "winter" came to an end.

The "little deaf woman from Norwich," as Lord Brougham referred to her, was to become one of the most prolific and influential intellectuals of her time.

Notes

1. Harriet's family included: Elizabeth (1794–1850), who married Thomas Greenhow, a surgeon at Newcastle-on-Tyne; Thomas (1795–1826), also a surgeon, married Helen Bourne, died early of consumption; Henry (1797–1844), a bachelor businessman; Robert (1798–1874) married Jane Smith and had a brass foundry in Birmingham; Rachel Ann (1800–1878) unmarried, ran a young ladies' school in Liverpool; Harriet (1802–1876); James (1805–1900) married Helen Higginson and became a Unitarian minister, scholar,

and principal of Manchester College; and Ellen (1811–1889) married Alfred Higginson, a surgeon in Liverpool. David Martineau, *Pedigrees of the Martineau Family*, revised and continued by C. Anthony Crofton (1972).

2. Mrs. Martineau compensated for her limited education by her enthusiasm for and interest in literature and history which she was able to satisfy by "snatches of reading" and the "habit of adding to her store of knowledge," according to her daughter Ellen. Cited in Drummond, *The Life and Letters of James Martineau*, 1:9.

3. Harriet was frightened by reflections of sunlight or lamplight. She cites incidents when she could not see the sea, or the comet of 1811, and was ridiculed by other members of the family. She had no explanation for these anxieties and their effects. She blamed herself for much of her personal suffering: "I have no doubt I was an insufferable child for gloom, obstinacy and crossness" (*Auto.*, 1:43). Her brother James comments that "Harriet's ultimate mood and estimates of things transformed and distorted her seeming memories of early life" (Drummond 1902, 1:8).

4. Although it is difficult to assess the veracity of Harriet's negative experiences apart from her own interpretations, the memories of childhood were impressive and still powerful when she wrote her Autobiography in her fifties. As she notes, she did receive, at rather critical points, encouragement, support, and constructive help from her family, especially Thomas, James, and even her mother.

   Her *Autobiography* reveals that considerable personal growth resulted from learning to cope with deafness and generally poor health. In several publications she provides insights and suggestions for coping with health problems, as in her essay "Letter to the Deaf" published in 1834 and *Life in the Sickroom* (1844). See also her *Autobiography*, 1:13, 72–78.

5. Robert K. Webb, *Harriet Martineau: A Radical Victorian*. (New York: Columbia University Press, 1960), 78–80. Vera Wheatley, *The Life and Work of Harriet Martineau*. (London: Secker & Warburg, 1957), especially Chapter Two.

SUMMER

2 The Inveterate Educator

> A soul there is, as pure as thou and rare;
> 'Midst heartless crowd in solitude she dwells;
> Conscious that kindred spirits breathe afar,
> And cheer'd by that prophetic hope which tells
> That flowers shall spring where now no promise
>   shows,
> And e'en this desert "blossom like the rose."
> —"The Flower of the Desert," 1830

As a young woman Harriet Martineau was keenly aware of her solitude, created in part by her increasing deafness and in part by her desire to become an author, a voice in society. She was convinced that there were indeed kindred spirits who searched for understanding and direction. It was to those kindred spirits – her readership – that she dedicated her life's work.

From the beginning of her writing career in 1822, Harriet Martineau assumed the role of educator. Even her earliest articles have a didactic quality which became the hallmark of her writings. As a daughter of the Enlightenment, committed to social progress and human perfectibility, Martineau became convinced of the power of education by the writings of Locke and Hartley. Her own experience had demonstrated to her the power of the mind in self-formation and of books and ideas in coping with the world.

Begun in 1805 by the Reverend Robert Aspland, the *Monthly Repository* was an important forum for Dissenters and other middle-class intellectuals in a rapidly changing and rather tense industrial England.[1] From 1826 to 1837 under the editorship and subsequent ownership of William J. Fox, Unitarian minister of South Place Chapel in London and foreign secretary of the Unitarian Association, many influential writers of the era, including J.S. Mill, Robert Browning, Richard Henry Horne, James Martineau, William Bridges, Harriet Hardy Taylor, and John James Tayler, contributed to the *Monthly Repository*.[2]

21

Harriet's first publications indicate her self-consciousness as a woman writer. She chose to write and submit her work in secret, to use, as many women did, a male pseudonym, Discipulus (and later H.M., V., D.F.), and to focus, at least initially, on the subject of women. Her first article, "Female Writers on Practical Divinity," published in two parts in the October and December 1822 issues of the *Monthly Repository*, praised the writings of gifted English female authors on the subject of Christian conduct. The articles drew attention to the distinctive contributions of the female perspective on Christian life and communication. Although she had reservations about considerable portions of Hannah More's theology, Martineau recommended her *Practical Piety*, particularly for its emphasis on Christian conduct and the significance of humans' influence upon one another in eliciting virtue in others or in setting a virtuous example. Her praise for the important contemporary female poet Anna Laetitia Barbauld centered on Barbauld's "Essay on the Inconsistency of Human Expectations" which examined religion "as a system of opinions, . . . a principle regulating the conduct, . . . as a taste, in which sense it is properly called devotion."[3]

Martineau's second essay, "On Female Education," in February 1823, was feminist in its theme and reminiscent of the work of Mary Wollstonecraft. In it Harriet emphasized that women's abilities could not be fully utilized without proper education and that the differences between men and women were, in the main, related to the differences in educational opportunities.

She discussed three traditional objections to the enlightening of the female mind: that women would neglect their duties; that their achievements would never equal those of men; and that knowledge would enhance women's vanity and cause them to forget their subordinate position (*MR*, 18:78). She pointed out that the duties of women were comparatively mean occupations, easily learned and performed; they were not enough to absorb a woman's time or her mental energies. Like Mary Wollstonecraft in 1791, Martineau appealed to male vanity by arguing that women who were ignorant creatures of domesticity could not be proper companions to men. Like Wollstonecraft before her and Charlotte Perkins Gilman and Olive Schreiner after her, Martineau maintained that enlightened motherhood requires proper education and a developed mind. More importantly, greater equity in the development of the sexes would result in androgyny of intellectual and moral virtue:

> When this is done, when woman is allowed to claim her privileges as an intellectual being, the folly, the frivolity, and all the mean vices and faults which have hitherto been the reproach of the sex, will gradually disappear. As . . . her rank in the scale of being is elevated, she will engraft the vigorous qualities of the mind of man on her own blooming virtues, and insinuate into his mind those softer graces and milder beauties, which will smooth the ruggedness of his character. Surely this is the natural state of things, and to this perfection will they arrive, if the improvement of the female mind proceeds with the same rapidity which we have now reason to anticipate (ibid., 81).

Martineau's most important contributions to the *Monthly Repository* appeared between 1826 and 1831, under the editorship of William J. Fox. Martineau's relationship with Fox was one of the most significant of her career. She first wrote to him in November of 1828 in response to his advertisement for "voluntary assistance to render the work a worthy organ," offering her participation, although she had been an occasional contributor since 1822. In their correspondence, which lasted until 1857, Martineau and Fox discussed the work of the *Monthly Repository*, Martineau's writings (particularly the political economy series), a wide range of issues and current affairs, Fox's controversial relationship with his ward and secretary Eliza Flowers and Harriet's assessment of it, and personal experiences.[4]

In her *Autobiography* she acknowledged Fox's literary tutorship as well as the gentleness, respect, and courtesy shown her by both Fox and his friends. Other than her younger brother James, Fox was the most important influence on Martineau during this period of her life. "His editorial correspondence with me was unquestionably the occasion, and in great measure the cause, of the greatest intellectual progress I ever made before the age of thirty" (*Auto.*, 1:140).

The 1820s brought a mix of encouraging and traumatic events to Harriet Martineau. The joy of seeing her first articles published in the *Monthly Repository* in 1822 and 1823 was tempered by her increasing deafness, to which she responded with a heightened sense of the responsibility of the deaf not to be a burden to others. In this decade there were several deaths in Harriet's family. Her brother Thomas, searching for relief from a respiratory illness, traveled to Madeira with his wife and infant son, but the baby died soon after their arrival, and Thomas followed in June 1824. Thomas Martineau, Sr., devastated by the death of his eldest son, died in June 1826. His daughter described her father as a "humble, simple, upright, self-denying, affectionate man who would not harm another and sacrificed all for his family" (*Auto.*, 1:127). During this trying time Harriet's own health suffered when, in addition to her permanent hearing disability and a liver ailment, she developed a "digestive derangement" which plagued her for at least four years and recurred later in life. Nevertheless, these family crises seemed to make her feel useful and closer to other family members. Death affected Harriet in another important relationship.

In 1823 James brought home John Hugh Worthington, a fellow student from college, who became infatuated with Harriet on his first visit. Some time later Worthington, by then a Unitarian minister, asked for Harriet's hand, and she, acting on convention rather than affection, accepted. They became engaged in 1826. She later recalled her great anxiety rather than elation in the anticipation of having to take responsibility for another's happiness. Perhaps Martineau already saw herself as a strong and increasingly self–sufficient person who might have to bolster up someone far less so. It is quite likely that she anticipated her growing autonomy and strength of character would be threatened by marriage. Just as Harriet was convincing herself that she could find love and happiness in marriage, her fiancé fell ill, went mad, and died within the year. Perhaps as an act of self-protection, Martineau distanced herself from his illness and his family; in fact, she refused to visit him and requested the return of her letters. She recovered quickly from the death of her fiancé in May 1827 and within a month was in "high spirits."

Because she suffered from a fear of inadequacy regarding the responsibilities of marriage and motherhood, Martineau never regretted or grieved her lost chance of marriage. Her strong belief in the importance of domestic life and her disillusionment at the rarity of its perfection convinced her that marriage was only for the strong and the brave. Unpleasant childhood memories probably played their part. She later realized "that there is a power of attachment in me that has never been touched," but, given "the serious and irremediable evils and disadvantages of married life, as it exists among us at this time," the only choice she saw for herself was "substantial, laborious and serious occupation." So, she resolved to choose the single life and in retrospect wrote:

> I am not only entirely satisfied with my lot, but think it the very best for me, – under my constitution and circumstances: and I long ago came to the conclusion that, without meddling with the case of the wives and mothers, I am probably the happiest single woman in England (*Auto.*, 1:133).

In fact, there seems little doubt that Harriet was relieved and even exhilarated by the termination of the obligation to marry. Throughout her life she had many male friends and acquaintances, including Erasmus Darwin, Henry Crabb, Robinson, Henry Reeve and a particularly interesting relationship with Henry George Atkinson. But she preferred to live alone or with other women, and to dedicate herself to work rather than to love.

By her early twenties Martineau was driven by the desire to write, and she wanted nothing to interfere with that. Nothing ever did. In 1855 she wrote:

> My business in life has been to think and learn, and to speak out with absolute freedom and what I have thought and learned . . . My work and I have been fitted to each other, as is proved by the success of my work and my own happiness in it. The simplicity and independence of this vocation first suited my infirm and ill-developed nature, and then sufficed for my needs, together with family ties and domestic duties, such as I have been blessed with, and as every woman's heart requires (*Auto.*, 1:133).

During the period 1826–31 Martineau wrote religious stories, developing them into such books as *Traditions of Palestine* (1830), and *Five Years of Youth; or, Sense and Sentiment* (1831). She also wrote three prize-winning essays for a contest whose purpose was to introduce Unitarianism to Catholics, Jews, and

Mohammedans (1831–32). Harriet submitted these essays separately and anonymously, each handwritten by another to disguise the author. She won the prize in each of the three competitions. Her interests in philosophy, literature, and science continued to grow, and from 1826 to 1831 Martineau contributed over one hundred stories, reviews, philosophical and moral essays, parables and poems to the *Monthly Repository*. Many of these were republished in Boston by Hilliard, Gray and Company in 1836 in two volumes entitled *Miscellanies*.[5]

These writings reflect the Christian vision of the early Harriet Martineau, although she increasingly wrote about the role of philosophy and the moral sciences in the pursuit of human improvement and social progress, concerns which reflected her educational and family background. However, by the late 1830s and 1840s she was criticizing religion as a source of oppression and narrowness and emphasizing the increasing role of the moral sciences in directing human conduct. Martineau interpreted her own intellectual evolution in terms of the positivist Law of Three Stages – the transformation of thought from the theological to the philosophical to the scientific – emphasized by Saint-Simon and Auguste Comte, both of whom she read and integrated into her own thinking. This law understood the transformation of modern Western mind and society to have begun in the theological stage, in which the natural world and life in society were interpreted within a religious, usually Christian, framework and change was believed to be exercised by the gods or God. This evolved into a stage of metaphysical or philosophical interpretation of the world and history which reflected human beings' increasing proclivity for rational logical explanation and theories based on general principles or abstract systems. The third stage, the scientific stage, had emerged from the second, and emphasized concrete, factual, 'verifiable' knowledge based on direct empirical exploration of the natural and social worlds.

Martineau's intellectual inspiration came from several sources. Unitarianism had provided her with exposure to the English intellectual and cultural heritage and an appreciation for education. She had become familiar with some of the leading thinkers of the day through personal contact (D'Eichtal, Malthus, Fox, Carpenter) and through reading (Priestley, Montesquieu, Locke, Lessing). Necessarianism and natural law theory were incorporated into her thinking, as she read Priestley's treatment of the associationism of David Hartley and the writings of Dugald Stewart, a Baconian and important natural law theorist.[6] The Enlightenment principle of the unity of the laws of nature and the laws of social life became the basis of positive philosophy toward which rationalists such as Martineau were drawn. Political economy, which expressed the workings of immutable principles in industrial capitalist society, had attracted Martineau as a student of Mr. Perry and became an increasingly important topic for her during the *Monthly Repository* years.

On the issues of natural rights, liberty, and equality, Martineau took the liberal Unitarian view. In harmony with William Godwin she extolled a vision of a democratic society which enshrines freedom and natural rights. Recognizing Godwin's concern over the barriers to self-realization created by inequalities in society, she showed the link between the fate of the individual and change in society:

> It is no region in the clouds that we are contemplating; it is a land of promise stretched out before our eyes, in all its distinct reality. The prophetic voice of philanthropy has long announced to us a state of society in which every individual shall be employed according to his capacity, and rewarded according to his works: and in the meanwhile we are ready to hail the appearance of any 'Thoughts on Man', which ... suggest means for securing to him all his rights, and cultivating all his capabilities (*Miscellanies*, "Godwin's Thoughts on Man," 2:132).

As a young woman Martineau had been passionately committed to the idea of progress in society and the utilitarian goal of individual well-being; her commitment was tempered only by an unshakable belief in "eternal and irreversible laws, working in every department of the universe, without any interference from any random will, human or divine" (*Auto.*, 1:111). This philosophy suggested not fatalism but the importance of individual responsibility and action. As early as 1832 she emphasized the fact that members of society must learn and be guided by the natural principles of the social order. In a review of Thomas Cooper's *Lectures on the Elements of Political Economy* she said:

> Viewing this science as we do, – as involving the laws of social duty and social happiness, – we hold it as a positive obligation on every member of society who studies and reflects at all, to

inform himself of its leading principles. If he cares at all about the faithful discharge of his functions in the position he holds, he must feel himself obliged to learn what those functions are, and how they may be best discharged (*Miscellanies*, "On the Duty of Studying Political Economy," 1:276).

In 1830 Martineau was introduced to the work of the French sociologist Saint-Simon by the French socialist Gustav D'Eichtal, who was visiting William Fox in England at the time. She became enthusiastic about French positivism.[7] Saint-Simon's ideas on the progressive evolution of society, the positivist basis for knowledge and social reorganization, and the organic nature of society appeared in her later writings.

In an 1829 review she wrote:

A world of truth is before us. We cannot help desiring to explore it; and we know of no interdiction which need exclude us from any part of it. We ought, therefore, to disregard the mistaken advice and impotent threats which would deter us, and press forward to the limits of science, determined to ascertain for ourselves where we must stop, and to heed no prohibition but that of Nature, or of Him who constituted Nature (*Miscellanies*, "Crombie's Natural Theology," 2:167).

Martineau clarified her view on the relation of truth and society: "We have no clear conceptions of truth otherwise than as an object of reason arrived at by a process of induction" (*Miscellanies*, "Theology, Politics and Literature," 1:193).

For a considerable time she had seen the principles of philosophy and science as confirmations of the basic Christian moral code and the Word of God as she learned it in Unitarian chapel. In 1824 she still believed

that the ultimate truths of revelation were revealed by God; that science has since developed a train of reasoning which, by leading to the same conclusions, at once corroborates their correctness, strengthens our faith, and demonstrates its own truth. Hence there can be no ground for the fear that this theory [Hartley's] should lead us away from scripture; it is derived from scripture; it pursues the same path (*Monthly Repository*, "Defense of Metaphysical Studies," xix:269).

However, by 1829 Martineau's "Essays on the Art of Thinking" in the *Monthly Repository* reflected her growing attraction to scientific positivism. Intended to champion "the noble faculty of reason," the essays presented the ideas of Newton, Bacon, and Locke to show both the errors and the new ideas influencing the progress of science and rationality in everyday life.[8] The essays emphasized the interdependence of mind and heart, of rationality and instrumentality. Moral strength and intellectual strength coincide and are developed by duty, progress, and work. Martineau concluded that not only will intellectual activity provide the power to cope with life's difficulties and challenges, but also those who are enlightened will enjoy a favored place with God.[9]

The year 1829 was the "Janus of Winter and Summer" for Harriet Martineau. Her digestive troubles persisted, and she went to Newcastle for successful treatment by her brother-in-law, Thomas M. Greenhow. The death in Norwich of her cousin James Martineau Lee brought her aged aunt to live with the Martineaus. But the most significant event of the year was the failure in June of the family manufactory which had been ailing since the speculations and subsequent economic crash of 1825 and 1826. The event was not lost on Harriet Martineau, who took a dim view of the speculative and greedy use of money and praised those who earned it through hard work.

The collapse of the family business was a calamity:

> My mother and her daughters lost, at a stroke, nearly all they had in the world by the failure of the house, – the old manufactory, – in which their money was placed. We never recovered more than the merest pittance; and at the time, I, for one, was left destitute; – that is to say, with precisely one shilling in my purse (*Auto.*, 1:141).

But with financial disaster came an opportunity to reexamine options and, as she put it, to act rather than simply to endure. This second turning point in Harriet's young life loosened her from the shackles of class which had threatened her independence and aspirations.

> I, who had been obliged to write before breakfast, or in some private way, had henceforth liberty to do my own work in my own way; for we had lost our gentility. Many and many a time

29

since have we said that, but for that loss of money, we might have lived on in the ordinary provincial method of ladies with small means, sewing, and economizing, and growing narrower every year; whereas, by being thrown, while it was yet time, on our own resources, we have worked hard and usefully, won friends, reputation and independence, seen the world abundantly, abroad and at home, and, in short, have truly lived instead of vegetated (*Auto.*, 1:142).

But what was she to do, being too handicapped by deafness to be employed as a governess, the main occupation for single middle-class women? It was agreed that she, her mother and aunt would remain in the family house, while her sisters sought outside employment. Harriet tried various schemes, including a correspondence course for young women on religion, philosophy, political economy, and literature (for which she received no applications), and made an attempt to publish an historical novel about John Howard, but without success. Finally, she took up sewing for about a year and lived on a fifty pounds income during that period.

It was at this time that she asked Fox for payment for her contributions to the *Monthly Repository*. To help her Fox sent a packet of nine books to review and agreed to pay her fifteen pounds per year. "Here was, in the first place, work; in the next, continued literary discipline under Mr. Fox; and lastly, this money would buy my clothes. So to work I went, with needle and pen" (*Auto.*, 1:145).

Harriet who had begun to study German now found new inspiration in German literature: "It was truly *life* that I lived during those days of strong intellectual and moral effort" (ibid.). While life was difficult – needlework during the short daylight hours of winter to provide what income there was, literary work starting after tea and often continuing until two or three o'clock in the morning, yet managing to obey the rule to be present at breakfast at eight – Harriet was happy in anticipation of new possibilities. These were accompanied, however, by anxiety and intense seriousness. A visit to London to see Fox and to try, in vain, to sell some articles yielded the offer of a low paying, proof-correcting job. But Mrs. Martineau ordered Harriet back to Norwich to fill the place vacated by her younger sister Ellen, who went out to work as a governess. At twenty-seven Harriet was not yet independent.

The intellectual interests and ideas which Martineau expressed in her articles for the *Monthly Repository* increasingly centered around political economy, and she began to write stories about economic and social issues. Perhaps most central to her ideas was Adam Smith's "identity of interests," which assumed that the goals of society would be served by the pursuit of the self-interests of individual members. Martineau's urge to communicate to the general public the "natural principles" operating in society increased as she became convinced that such understanding would promote social progress.

Martineau claimed that her first secular writings were quite unintentionally in political economy. In 1827 she was contributing occasional "little eightpenny stories" (for which she was paid two to five pound each) for publication by Houlston in Shropshire, when she decided to write a story about recent machine-breaking. *The Rioters*, written in the first person male, focused on the problems of a changing division of labor, on the futility and unlawfulness of machine destruction and the need for people to acquire a variety of useful and salable skills. When a story on wages was requested by "some hosiers and lace-makers of Derby," Martineau produced *The Turn Out; or, Patience the Best Policy*, which asserted that strikes ruin the lives of workers, and that wages cannot exceed the rate of profit.

These tales were well received, and Houlston asked Martineau to write "a good many tracts." When, in the autumn 1827, Harriet picked up a copy of Jane Marcet's *Conversations on Political Economy*,

> great was my surprise to find that I had been teaching [Political Economy] unawares, in my stories about Machinery and Wages. It struck me at once that the principles of the whole science might be advantageously conveyed in the same way, – not by being smothered up in a story, but be being exhibited in their natural workings in selected passages of social life. It has always appeared very strange to me that so few people seem to have understood this. Students of all manner of physical sciences afterwards wanted me to "illustrate" things of which social life (and therefore fiction) can afford no illustration. I used to say till I was tired that none but moral

and political science admitted of the method at all (*Auto.*, 1:138).

In 1831 Martineau used the prize money from the essays on Unitarianism to visit her brother James and his wife in Dublin, where James was minister of the Unitarian church on Eustace Street. There she made the decision to write a series of stories illustrating the principles of political economy.[10] Martineau began the 25-volume *Illustrations of Political Economy* in 1832 with resolve and her typical sense of duty toward her work, a "thorough, well-considered, steady conviction that the work was wanted, – even craved by the popular mind" (*Auto.*, 1:160).

Martineau was convinced that public education was both desired and needed for progress in society. Indeed, her struggles to publish her writings, to cope with exploitation by publishers, and to attempt to support herself as a professional writer were tolerable only because of her passion and determination.

Martineau's solitude was most apparent in the months during which she prepared for the series. She approached several publishers; two in Dublin refused to consider her proposal for the series on the grounds that other issues such as the status of the Reform Bill and the cholera epidemic were distracting the public mind. Baldwin and Cradock in London wished to impose their own views on her work, even insisting that the words political economy not be used, and finally wrote that, once again, "considering the public excitement about the Reform Bill and the Cholera, they dared not venture" (*Auto.*, 1:163). Other publishers withdrew for similar reasons.

In the chilling days of early December 1831 Martineau made her way by coach to London to stay with her cousin Richard, a partner at Whitbread's Brewery. Trudging the streets of London in gloomy weather, calling on publishers by day and writing at night, Martineau finally broke into tears at Fox's house. The following day Fox's brother, Charles, offered to publish her work, but his terms were harsh. Five hundred subscriptions, provided by both parties, were to be obtained before publication would begin; Fox was to have half the profits besides the usual commission and privileges, and the agreement could cancelled after any five numbers. As Charles Fox had no connections or money at the time, Martineau saw that the responsibility for the success of the project would depend entirely on her. In addition, she received discouraging comments from several people who scolded her for her rashness in such a proposal. James Mill told Fox that he was convinced that Martineau's method of explication could not succeed. (Two years later Mill acknowledged his mistake.) After an argument, Charles Fox issued Harriet an ultimatum – a thousand copies of the first two numbers must be sold in a fortnight! Although weary and discouraged, doubtful even of William Fox's support, Martineau nevertheless resolved to push ahead. As she wrote her Preface one night, the clock struck two:

> I thought of the multitudes who needed it, – and especially of the poor, – to assist them in managing their own welfare. I thought too of my own conscious power of doing this very thing. Here was the thing wanting to be done, and I wanting to do it; and the one person who had seemed to best under-stand the whole affair now urged me to give up either the whole scheme, or, what was worse, its main principle! ... I cried in bed till six, when I fell asleep; but I was at the breakfast table by half-past eight, and ready for the work of the day (*Auto.*, 1:171–72).

At this point support from her relatives, particularly in the form of subscriptions, became a great source of encourage-ment. Her mother suggested that Harriet send copies of the prospectus for the series to every member of Parliament. The Gurneys of the Norwich banking family offered to help Harriet and asked to be consulted before any decision to give up the project. Although up to the week of publication subscriptions were low, the public response was immediate and clear: Harriet's tales became an astonishing success. Newspapers, periodicals, and letters proclaimed their support for Harriet's work. The Society for the Diffusion of Useful Knowledge, which had re-jected one of her tales, now wanted to publish the series; there were other offers of purchase. Members of Parliament sent her blue books (i.e., parliamentary publications on various mat-ters), and her incoming mail outgrew the delivery capacity of the local post office.

The critical indicator of success was the number of sales, 1,500 for the first number and by 1834 an average of 10,000 copies per month. This can be compared with the sales of other well-known authors of the period: J.S. Mill's *Principles* sold 3,000 copies in four years; Dickens's novels, which had been serialized first, had a sale of 2,000 or 3,000 copies and were considered very successful; at its height, the *Edinburgh Review*, to which Harriet was soon to become a contributor, had a circulation of 13,000 (Blaug 1958, 129). She seems to have outsold nearly everyone.[11] Recognizing that it had become important to be in London to attend to her research and publishing affairs, Harriet moved there in November 1832. Ten months later she bought a house on Fludyer Street, Westminster, which she shared with her mother and aunt until 1839 when poor health caused Harriet to leave London altogether.

Although the author's original plan for the political economy series was to publish one tale per quarter, at the insistence of her publisher and her brother James, Harriet committed herself to a story per month, for a total of twenty-three stories in twenty-five parts. While writing this series she was convinced by Charles Fox to extend the series with some tales on taxation, subsequently *Illustrations of Taxation* (1834). In the meantime, she was urged by Lord Brougham, on behalf of the Society for the Diffusion of Useful Knowledge, to do a series of tales on the Poor Laws, *Poor Laws and Paupers* (1833–34). It is not surprising that two-and-a-half years of preparing and writing stories on an unalterable schedule precipitated health problems and exhaustion.

The rigorous schedule required organization and industriousness, and Martineau developed a procedure for research and writing.[12] She later recalled: "Authorship has never been with me a matter of choice. I have not done it for amusement, or for money, or for fame, or for any reason but because I could not help it" (*Auto.*, 1:188–89).

In her philosophy of writing she maintained that literary labor is much like any other toil. She had "suffered, like other writers, from indolence, irresolution, distaste to my work, absence of 'inspiration,' and all that." But, she wrote:

> I have also found that sitting down, however reluctantly, with the pen in my hand, I have never worked for one quarter of an hour without finding myself in full train; so that all the quarter hours, arguings, doubtings, and hesitation as to whether I should work or not which I gave way to in my inexperience, I now regard as so much waste, not only of time but, far worse, of energy (*Auto.*, 1:190–91).

Martineau maintained that writing must become a habit, to be done in the best hours of the day and as free as possible from interruption. "I never pass a day without writing; and the writing is always done in the morning" (*Auto.*, 1:191). Because she was so serious about her work, it structured her life in a routine, disciplined way. At home or away, her schedule was the same: a morning wash, a long walk, breakfast, work in undisturbed solitude from 7:30 or 8:00 AM until 2:00 PM, socializing in the afternoon and evening, correspondence and occasional writing in the late hours, four to five hours sleep. And, although she was occasionally obliged to "work double tides," she never made it a practice.

Martineau's entire purpose in writing the political economy series was public education. Her aim was to furnish information about the economic and social laws operating in society within a context meaningful to the average (middle- and working-class) reader in an economical and physically accessible format. Martineau did not claim to be either an economist or a particularly original writer, but she was highly skilled in reducing the principles of a new science to a popular form. For the first series, she relied on sources by James Mill, Smith, Malthus, and Steward. Mill's *Elements of Political Economy* (1821), which presented David Ricardo's principles of the science in the popular "school-book" form, had been criticized for being too abstract and unappealing to the public. By following Mill's systematic organization of principles but presenting them in fictional contexts, Martineau accomplished what Mill was unable to do, make political economy accessible to the ordinary individual.

Like Mill, the young author organized her "political economy for the people" into four divisions: production, distribution, exchange, and consumption, with subdivisions where appropriate. She also obtained "all the standard works . . . of what I then took to be a science" (*Auto.*, 1:193). She noted her own ideas on the subject and then read and took notes from her scientific sources. (Years later she commented on how undeveloped the discipline was then.)

The themes and issues woven into the thirty-four novelettes, which includes those on political economy, taxation and Poor Laws, involve the significant economic and social debates of the time. Martineau's intention was to present simple, didactic stories

35

comprehensible to all classes – "all classes bear an equal relation to the science" (Preface, I:xiv).

While she did not shun controversial and complex issues, she was nevertheless criticized for oversimplification and incautiousness in her direct approach. Her analysis, portrayed in fiction, reflected a view of society in which the increasing division of labor magnified the interdependence of the social classes. She seemed to agree with Herbert Spencer that complex societies are more vulnerable precisely because of this interdependence. Hence the duty of members of all classes to understand the principles and relationships of the complex social organism became ever more crucial. The fate of each was the fate of all.

> If it concerns rulers that their measures should be wise, if it concerns the wealthy that their property should be secure, the middling classes that their industry should be rewarded, the poor that their hardships should be redressed, it concerns all that Political Economy should be understood. If it concerns all that the advantages of a social state should be preserved and improved, it concerns them likewise that Political Economy should be understood *by all* (ibid., xvi).

This meant, of course, that political economy must be written not only for the learned but for everyone in order to enhance happiness and progress in society.

> *Sciences are only valuable in as far as they involve the interests of mankind at large, and . . . nothing can prevent their sooner or later influencing general happiness.* This is true with respect to the knowledge of the stars; to that of the formation and changes of the structure of the globe; to that of chemical elements and their combinations; and, above all, to that of the social condition of men. . . . the first eminent book on this new science [is] Smith's Wealth of Nations . . . but [it] is not fitted nor designed to teach the science to the great mass of the people (ibid., ix–x. Emphasis added).

While later critics and biographers regarded the series as contributions to fiction rather than lessons in economics, for Martineau fiction was to be the vehicle, the means, to public education. In the preface she made it clear that her choice of locations and characters was meant to reflect principles and evolution of a universal system, and each story was followed by a

36

summary of the principles illustrated therein to make the meaning and purpose of the story very clear. Originally each book was published separately in small paperback editions ($3\frac{3}{4}$ x $5\frac{3}{4}$ inches), to be put in a pocket or a lunch carrier for leisure reading at any opportunity. The nearly simultaneous publication of the twenty-five stories in nine, leather-bound volumes was intended to appeal to the middle classes. The volume of sales would indicate that the stories were read by middle and working classes alike.

The topics in the tales included: labor as the basis of wealth and capital; the growing division of labor and the effects of machinery; the relation between wages, prices, and profits; the importance of individual initiative and labor and the negative effects of state support; the necessity to limit population growth; the principles of a market economy and free competition; supply and demand; the function and supply of money; the advantages of free trade; the positive and negative roles played by unions; productive and unproductive consumption; the requirement of public expenditure for defense, public order, and social improvement; the importance of just taxation and the need to avoid public indebtedness.

The first tale concerning the subject of production is *Life in the Wilds*, set in rural South Africa where some Europeans are invaded by Bushmen and lose all their worldly possessions plus a few lives. Being forced to reestablish their livelihoods, the newcomers' discussions and ultimate action reflect their realization that labor is the basis of all wealth and that proprieties of rank are useless and impede social and economic progress.

In the second tale, *The Hill and the Valley*, set in an ironworks in South Wales, the relationships between labor, capital, and technology are explored. The fundamental message is that the welfare of the worker depends on his/her willingness to adjust to increasing differentiation in the division of labor created particularly by new machinery and the new investments of capital. Again in *Brooke and Brooke Farm*, which concerns the consequences of the enclosures, the new division of labor is seen to reflect the expanding manufacturing and commerce sectors. However, the story stresses the importance of agricultural capital and the interdependence of these segments of the economy.

Particular tales in this series are worth examining in some detail, because of their quality as stories or as portrayals of certain social and economic issues and because of their impact on Martineau's readers. One such story, *Demarara*, set on a tropical island in the West Indies, concerns the institution of slavery, which is viewed as incompatible with good capitalism and free trade. In this tale good morals make for good economics. Protectionism leads to the ruin of land, labor and production. Additionally, natural right dictates that one man cannot hold another as property, as Alfred Bruce, the British-educated plantation son, observes. Property must be consistent with the general good. Alfred concludes that the consequences of slavery include the slaves' cruelty to each other and to the animals, as well as their own self-deprecation. Slavery leads to the ultimate ruination of all. Alfred's education, he realizes, has ruined him as a planter. In the story, justice, or at least revenge, is served when the cruel, white foreman Horner is drowned in a hurricane, but several slaves also suffer death by bloodhounds, separation, and abuse by other slaves.

The plight of slaves as a whole is bad, but women slaves are thoroughly abused and exploited, by whites and by other slaves, as confirmed by Hester's experiences of abuse since the age of ten. "Slavery is the school of tyranny."

> A white woman has nobody to rule her but her husband, and nobody can hurt her without his leave; but a slave's wife must obey her master before her husband, and he cannot save her from being flogged (*Demarara*, 61).

In the tale Martineau proffers slavery as utterly uneconomical from a political economy standpoint and a waste of resources of all kinds, leading, among other things, to the depreciation of the soil through overfarming (a Malthusian idea). She makes the case for free labor as more productive than slave labor for wages and task work over endless labor. Fair wages paid to workers who have a share in the system accomplish far more than the lack of reward for the oppressed in a despotic economy. The solution involves the controversial American Colonization Scheme, designed to send negroes back to Africa, which Martineau only later, following her visit to America, recognized to be a reactionary solution to slavery. Although her purpose was to illustrate economic principles, the inhumanity of slavery is also predominant in this story, which established her reputation as an abolitionist.

Martineau gave rather exquisite portrayals of character in some of her stories, perhaps nowhere as fine as Ella in *Ella of Garveloch* and *Weal and Woe in Garveloch*, tales V and VI, set in the Hebrides. With these stories Martineau moves to the second set of principles of political economy dealing with distribution. The theme was to do with land rent as related to capital, production, and prices. The beautiful, hard-working Ella raises her brothers and supports the family through fishing. Eventually her friend Angus, who has gone off to Canada, returns. They marry, and Angus goes into farming. In *Weal and Woe*, Garveloch and the other isles are sold to a fishing company, and a new economy and new opportunities emerge. Ella and Angus, their nine children, and the other inhabitants begin to prosper. The population increases significantly, and farm fields disappear as new homes as built. Unfortunately, a lower than expected crop yield results in the inhabitants consuming the products they were to sell. Competition for employment with the fish company increases as new families move in, and some, failing to recognize their shared interests, commit mean acts against others. The food supply continues to dwindle, causing illness, unemployment, trouble among the children, and domestic violence. Bad luck continues. Ella and Katie Cuthbert, a widow who has fared better than others partly because her family size is stable, have a long conversation about population growth and control. They observe that people must be responsible to society when considering marriage and that happiness does not depend on total wealth but on its proportion to the population. Martineau's theme was, of course, that people must understand the natural laws of the relation of population to the food supply. Population controls such as celibacy and war are discussed. Several boys enlist in the services as a means of gaining livelihood. Captain Forbes's antiwar opinion makes it clear that war is not an acceptable control, but perhaps, as Angus observes, a decline in the marriage rate is. Widow Katie and her dear friend Ronald decide to maintain a platonic friendship rather than marry and contribute to the population problem. The Malthusian message about inevitable population increase is more than clear.

Through all this Ella remains the stable moral force of Garveloch. Martineau express her view of this ideal woman – sensitive, self-sufficient, strong – in the closing lines:

Ella was the last of the family to show the marks of change. Her mind and heart were as remarkable for their freshness in age as they had been for their dignity in youth. Inured to early exertion and hardship, she was equal to all calls upon her energies of body and spirit. She was still seen, as occasion required, among the rocks, or on the sea, or administering her affairs at home. She was never known to plead infirmity, or to need forbearance, or to disappoint expectation. She had all she wanted in her husband's devotion to her and his home, and she distributed benefits untold from the rich treasury of her warm affections. She had, from childhood, filled a station of authority, and had never abused her power, but made it the means of living for others. Her power increased with every year of her life, and with it grew her scrupulous watchfulness over its exercise, till the same open heart, penetrating eye, and ready hand, which had once made her the sufficient dependence of her orphan brothers, gave her an extensive influence over the weal and woe of Garveloch (*Weal and Woe in Garveloch*, 139).

Martineau was criticized for recommending the untenable Malthusian solutions of late marriage and celibacy as population controls and for bringing up the matter of population control at all. Nevertheless, she did not avoid such controversial subjects. It should be noted that she later recognized, due to the influence of Francis Place, that birth control was the central issue in population growth.

In Tale VII, *A Manchester Strike*, wages and the question of workers' combinations (unions) and strikes constitute the focus. The issues are embodied in Allen, the main character, who becomes the union secretary and spokesperson, only to be accused ultimately by the union of selling the suit of clothes which they had provided for him. Martineau portrays the ambivalence of workers toward the strike. The women are generally against the 'turn-out'. Allen and Hare will only strike for the rights of the workers but are in general against such action. In Martineau's didactic style, Allen expresses her concerns:

Some change, and that a speedy one, there ought to be in the condition of the working classes: they cannot go on long labouring their lives away for a less recompense than good habitations, clothing and food. These form the very least sum of the just rewards of industry; whereas a multitude are pinched with the frosts of winter, live amidst the stench of unwholesome dwellings in summer, have nearly forgotten the taste of animal food, and even sigh for bread as a luxury. The question to be debated, and to be put on trial if necessary, – and I wish every master in Manchester was here to take down my words for his further consideration, is whether a social being has not a right to comfortable subsistence in return for his full and efficient labour (*A Manchester Strike*, 50).

Again, through Allen, Martineau states the case of unions:

Combination on our part is necessary from power being lodged unequally in the hands of individuals, and it is necessary for labourers to husband their strength by union, if it is ever to be balanced against the influence and wealth of capitalists. A master can do as he pleases with his hundred or five hundred workmen, unless they are combined (ibid., 50–51).

Nevertheless, Allen cautions that

Integrity must be our rule as much as liberty is our warrant and justice our end . . . Honour towards our masters is as necessary as fidelity to each other (ibid., 52).

Allen makes it clear that he and every man must keep the terms of the contract and make up time lost during the strike. In dialogues, several issues are analyzed, including the relation of wages to the labor supply and the impact of technology, which is seen as a boon for workers and employers. One of the employers describes the likely consequences of the strike and presents his solutions to the workers' problems: to live on present wages keeping respectability and ambition until better days, to prepare for fluctuations by contributing to a relief fund, to place their children in different occupations, and to discourage early marriage of their children. These are solutions which Martineau reiterated in many of her writings on economy. In this case the strike continues, the children are unemployed, family life deteriorates, and things get very bad for all. The

conclusion is that unions are fine for pursuing certain grievances and unfair practices but that strikes are counterproduc-
tive in wage disputes. The strike ends but many employees,
including Allen, are not rehired. He must become a street
cleaner while his children work in the factory. Martineau ends
the story with a plea to remember the identity of interests and
to act accordingly.

Cousin Marshall, the eighth tale, anticipates the Poor Law
tales in its critique of almsgiving and charity. The Malthusian
themes continue, but the real questions are how to reduce the
number of indigent ("capable persons who cannot [will not]
support themselves") and, particularly, how to prevent the poor
("those who can live by their industry even having only enough
to subsist") from falling into that category. Workhouses, which
Martineau later supported in place of outdoor work, are portrayed here as contributing to unproductive consumption, population increase, and decrease of capital. Poor Law rates (taxes)
artificially support and ultimately injure the poor and society,
she maintained. Again, she later changed her mind and, having
spent a night in a workhouse, proclaimed that they were not so
bad after all.

In Tale IX, *Ireland,* Martineau wanted to draw attention to
"the silent miseries of the cottier, the unpitied grievances of the
spirit-broken labourer . . . miseries protracted from generation
to generation" (*Ireland,* ii). She criticized those practices which
harmed the laborer and which placed a heavy burden on the
insufficient capital. She advocated the industrialization of agriculture and improvement in domestic economy, education, and
emigration as measures to change positively the economic situation in Ireland. Population growth must be proportionate to
capital. These proposals were accompanied by her criticism of
the imposition of an alien church on the Irish and her recom-
mendation that the New Poor Law not be extended to Ireland
because it would impose too great a burden on the already
fragile capitalist class there. Although she "never understood
Irish nationalism or the emotional side of the Irish question,"
Martineau attacked the complex issues with a desire for rational
solutions (Cf. Wolff). She wrote on Ireland in later years.

The other tales dealing with distribution included *Homes
Abroad,* which dealt with voluntary emigration and penal colonization; *For Each and For All,* an antisocialist tale which explores

the relation of wages and profits and which advocates free trade and lower public costs rather than a sharing of economic returns; *French Wines and Politics* on use value and exchange value; and *The Charmed Sea*, set in Russia, dealing with the function of money and supply and demand.

The next group of tales on exchange included the two-part *Berkeley the Banker* which reiterates the advantages of a money economy but shows the disruptive nature of speculation, a factor in the collapse of the Martineau manufactory. *Messrs. Vanderput and Shoek* and *The Loom and The Lugger* advocate free trade and free competition. *Sowers Not Reapers* establishes Martineau's anti-Corn Law position. She maintained that free import of corn would not only give relief to those who cannot afford corn at high prices but also would avoid the use of poor soils and thereby promote a better use of labor (a Malthusian-Smithian position). *Cinnamon and Pearls*, set in Ceylon, presents the case for free trade between the mother country and the colony, stressing the waste of resources and cultivation of expensive dependency of the colony which are inevitable in restrictive economic relationships – a lesson for the twentieth as well as the nineteenth century. The final story in this group, *A Tale of the Tyne*, illustrates the case for government noninterference in trading and employment, participation of companies in public utilities, and the need for patent laws to protect individuals.

The last group of tales illustrates the principles of consumption. *Briery Creek*, based upon the life of Joseph Priestley, one of Harriet's most hallowed protagonists, expounds on productive versus unproductive consumption, the principles of supply and demand, and their reciprocal effects. *The Three Ages*, set in sixteenth-century London, concerns Sir Thomas More. The theme here is that public expenditure for defense, public order, and social improvement should be limited to the necessary because such funds are unproductive. Government should give their expenditures the following priority: education, public works, government and legislation, law and justice, diplomacy, defense, and, finally, the dignity of the sovereign. *The Farrers of Budge-Row* foreshadows her series on taxation. She supports graduated income and property taxes and direct taxation over taxes on commodities. To Martineau, the grossest injustices of taxation are permanent government loans requiring interest payments and the transmission of the National Debt to posterity. The final tale XXV, *The Moral of Many Fables*, is a review and clarification of the principles illustrated in the twenty-five tales.

The tales on political economy are varied if pedantic; the plots are sometimes intriguing, and character portrayal, although stereotypical and mechanical, is in some instances sensitive and real. In later years Martineau said she could not bear to look at these stories, although she retained her appreciation for the project which brought her financial independence.

Although Martineau is generally seen to have taken the pro-capital perspective of nineteenth-century liberalism, even a casual reading of these tales reveals her recognition and, indeed, inclusion of both sides of the issues. She accepted the right and necessity of unions while deploring what she considered to be the regressive aspects of strikes. Her nominalist model of society and her economic perspective placed cooperation and identity of interests above all other considerations. In her view the kind of world in which she lived still contained the possibilities for a workable, interdependent, fair, and progressive economic system in which class antagonisms would be subdued by the benefits accruing to all.[13]

She defined her role as a popularizer of these scientific theories.

> It must be perfectly needless to explain what I owe to preceding writers on the science of which I have treated. Such an acknowledgment could only accompany a pretension of my own to have added something to the science – a pretension which I have never made . . . Great men must have their hewers of wood and drawers of water; and scientific discoverers must be followed by those who will popularise their discoveries. When the woodman finds it necessary to explain that the forest is not of his planting, I may begin to particularize my obligations to Smith and Malthus, and others of their high order (*The Moral of Many Fables*, vi).

The Poor Laws

Harriet Martineau's reputation had become well established upon the publication of the political economy tales. She had considerable influence on politicians, including Brougham, Althorp, Drummond, and Grey, on the "whiggish gentlemen of the press such as *Edinburgh* reviewers Jeffrey, Smith and Empson" (Pichanik, 69), as well as on public opinion. Of course, she was criticized in the *Quarterly Review* for taking up such a subject at all since she was a woman, and by the Tories for her stand on population control and welfare (ibid., 69–70).

Soon, her public influence was demonstrated in the matter of the state's response to poverty. As early as the seventeenth century, England had addressed the problem of the poor in society and had established the Act of 1601, whose intention it was to provide relief for the infirm in society. The Speenhamland Plan of 1795 implemented outdoor relief with payments to supplement wages lower than a standard which was related to the price of bread. The effects were lower wages, as employers relied on government to make up the difference, higher rates, declines in yeomen, agricultural unemployment, and higher food prices.[14]

In 1832 a royal commission was appointed to investigate the Poor Laws; their report showed convincingly that change was needed. At this time Martineau was approached by Chancellor Brougham to write some tales on the Poor Laws in anticipation of the report of the Poor Law Commission. Although exhausted from her work on the political economy tales, she decided to take up the task because she perceived the Old Poor Laws to be a "gangrene of the state" (*Auto.*, 1:219). In truth, her work was being used by the government to get the forthcoming Poor Law Act through Parliament. She was given an advance copy of the *Extracts* of the Commission's report and wrote the Poor Law stories for publication before the session of Parliament which was to act on the recommendations. Her efforts were successful in those terms.

The Poor Law Amendment Act of 1834 passed easily as politicians were all too aware of the resistance toward rising poor rates. A commission was established to oversee poor relief which emphasized centralized control, inspections, and rather bureaucratic administration. Most significantly, the approach toward the able-bodied poor had changed – outdoor relief was terminated and replaced by workhouses, inhumane institutions where families were separated and people were isolated by age and sex and endured hard labor, limited diets, harsh and undesirable existences.[15]

The Poor Law stories were followed immediately by the supplementary series entitled *Illustrations of Taxation*, where she used a similar format to assert her views of taxation, namely, that taxation should be equitable, graduated on the basis of income and property, and not applicable to consumer goods. Again, she attacked the idea of government borrowing on interest and the national debt.

On behalf of the Society for the Diffusion of Useful Knowledge she published the *Poor Laws and Paupers* tales, and, several years later, the *Guide to Service* series. Both reflect her growing sociological perspective on society and the social class system and, as well, provide insights into the thinking of her generation regarding the consequences of industrial capitalism and the proper measures to deal with them.

The success of these series of stories written to educate the public brought the end of Martineau's financial worries and the beginning of a fascinating career. She reflected upon it many years later:

> Each period of my life has had its trials and heart-wearing difficulties . . . but in none had the pains and penalties of life a more intimate connexion with the formation of character than in the one which closes here. And now the summer of my life was bursting forth without any interval of spring (*Auto.*, 1:180).

Notes

1. The early nineteenth century was a period of tension in England caused by the desires for political reform and religious freedom and by lingering government fears of the importation of the French revolution. The Corporation and Test Acts (not repealed until 1828) and the rules of church-related institutions excluded Dissenters from public office and from universities while exercising control over nonconformists in matters of registration, of marriage and burial. Dissenters were liable to prosecution until 1813; Roman Catholics, whose cause was taken up by many Unitarians including Harriet Martineau, suffered discrimination until 1829. The *Monthly Repository* served to keep its readership informed on

political affairs and the quest for liberal reform. The publication is therefore an interesting reflection of the thought of a generation on political, philosophical, and social issues.

2. See Mineka, Chapter 6.

3. Martineau quotes Barbauld at length on devotion but warns that there is still too much imagination and feeling in her approach, *MR*, xvii:748.

4. Martineau's letters to Fox are in the R.S. Speck Collection in the University of California, Berkeley, Library. The letters reveal a great deal about the process of writing the political economy series.

5. These particular volumes, requested by and dedicated to Americans (as a result of Martineau's stay there), have to do, she said in the preface, with the progress of worship. She referred to self-inquisition, the development of a spiritual conscience and finally a spiritual repose in which we become aware of God's omnipresence. It is to the philosophers and philanthropists that we look for an understanding of the processes of nature and the institutions of society, as they "interpret the mysteries of God and prove the ways of men . . . To them is appointed labour – irksome labour, in the guardianship of their race" (*Miscellanies*, 'Preface,' 1836, viii).

6. The doctrine of philosophical necessity emphasized the "importance of moral habits, the never-failing consequences of moral discipline." One should waste neither time nor powers, but employ one's powers on the improvement of the present, "for the present is his own; the past and the future are beyond his power" (*MR*, "Defense of Metaphysical Studies," May 1824, xix:272). Priestley, who studied and wrote about Hartley, was himself a great student of the Scriptures. At this time Martineau seemed convinced that this doctrine was compatible with Christian philosophy. Bacon, Hartley, and Priestley were probably the most significant scientific figures to Martineau, although the mix of intellectual influences is quite broad.

7. Transcript of letter, HM to James Martineau, March 24, 1831, Manchester College. "Harriet is full of St. Simonism and bids me set him [Fox] agoing upon it."

8. Martineau discussed a number of topics and principles of scientific positivism and the necessity to cultivate systematic mental practices. See the "Essays on the Art of Thinking", *Miscellanies* 2:57–121).

9. Ibid., Essay VI. We see that before the age of thirty Harriet Martineau posed many complex religious and philosophical issues in the context of this religious publication. She was rather typical of her generation. Diana Postlethwaite has shown that among Martineau's peers the movement toward science resulted from the unsatisfactory answers provided by orthodox religion, and other cultural forms, to the problems of society. Echoing the views of the French positivists, Martineau called for the promotion of the moral sciences, to be based on the paradigm of the natural sciences.

10. "During that reading, groups of personages rose up from the pages, and a procession of action glided through its arguments, as afterwards from the pages of Adam Smith, and all the other Economists. I mentioned my notion, I remember, when we were sitting at work, one bright afternoon at home. Brother James nodded assent: my mother said 'do it;' and we went to tea, unconscious what a great thing we had done since dinner" (*Auto.*, 1:138–39).
11. See Mark Blaug 1958, Chapter 7, for a good, concise review of Harriet's political economy tales.
12. After a morning or an evening's work at organizing theoretical ideas, Harriet outlined the "summary of principles" at the end of each tale – "the most laborious part of the work." And then she chose the location for the tale. Each character was to embody a principle and the action of the story was to convey the "mutual operation of these embodied principles" (*Auto.*, 1:193ff.). The story was structured within an hour or two and materials regarding location obtained from travel or topography books. The next step was to develop copious outlines of scenes, persons, and actions for each chapter. After that, "the story went off like a letter." She wrote approximately twelve pages of about thirty-three lines each a day. At the completion of a number, when possible, she took two days to rest (eight hours sleep per night) and to restore her strengths for the next tale. During that two years she received background source material from a variety of people and places. Not always agreeing with the well-meaning donor, she made her own evaluation of the material, as in the case of Elliott Cresson, who posed as an anti-slavery agent but who was promoting the American Colonization Scheme (ibid., 197).
13. The system based on private property, yielding profits in which presumably everyone could share, was accepted as the viable foundation of the nineteenth-century bourgeois world (Houghton, 1957).
14. See Webb 1968, 205–52; Himmelfarb 1983, Chapter VI.
15. This discussion is based particularly on accounts in Webb and Himmelfarb. Himmelfarb's *The Idea of Poverty: England in the Early Industrial Age* is an excellent account of the formation of the concept of "the poor" and the institutionalization of poverty, particularly as related to classical political economy and radical responses to it, fictional portrayals, and the sociological study of the urban poor and the working classes.

3 The Sociologist Abroad

I

All men are equal in their birth,
Heirs of the earth and skies;
All men are equal when that earth
Fades from their dying eyes.

VI

Ye great! renounce your earth-born pride,
Ye low! your shame and fear:
Live, as ye worship, side by side:
Your common claims revere.
                    —"The Fraternity of Man," 1829

Travels in America

In June 1833, while Martineau was in the midst of her political economy tales, she wrote to William J. Fox that she was being encouraged by Lord Henley to use the opportunity of a well-needed holiday to explore America for the benefit of British understanding. As she reports in her *Autobiography*, when she asked Henley to give her a good reason for such a trip, he replied:

> Whatever else may or may not be true about the Americans, it is certain that they have got at principles of justice and mercy in their treatment of the least happy classes of society which we should do well to understand. Will you not go, and tell us what they are (*Auto.*, 1:270)?

Whether speaking accurately for Lord Henley or not, she related that meditation on the proposal convinced her that she should go. And it was clear that travel would have more purpose than simply leisure.

> If I am spared to come back, this country shall know something more than it does of the principles of American institutions. I am tired of being kept foundering among the details which are all that a Hall and a Trollope can bring away; and it

49

is urged upon me by some of our philanthropists, that I should go and see for myself. – What I have said seems presumptuous. But the thing should be done, and I will do it (HM to William Tait, August 29, 1833, MS. Ogden 101, University College, London).

The decision to travel to America in 1834 as a respite from two-and-a-half years of intensive work marked the beginning of Martineau's sociological investigations. In spite of her claims that this was to be a trip for leisure, she became almost immediately interested in exploring the norms, values, and social patterns of American society.

Before she left Liverpool in August 1834, she managed to resist attempts by publishers to obligate her with offers of sizable advances to write a book. Although she claims not to have made the decision to publish her findings until after her return to England, she kept "a very ample journal" and, even more significantly, prepared a methodology for her investigation during the six-week journey across the Atlantic. The work provided her with the opportunity to organize her ideas and strategies in preparation for a very purposeful visit to America.

Martineau was prompted to write *How To Observe Morals and Manners* while on her way to America. In 1834 an editor had requested her to write a chapter on the subject of morals and manners for a series to be entitled "How To Observe." She agreed to do it, but before her return from America, the proposed project was cancelled. Later, at the request of Charles Knight, who had decided to turn the series into separate volumes, Martineau expanded and edited her draft, and in the spring of 1838 she completed the volume, "this tough piece of work, which required a good deal of reading and thinking" (*Auto.*, 2:118). The book includes discussions on methodology and a theoretical framework for studying a society. Martineau discusses at length the necessity to establish certain methods and principles of social investigation a priori. She emphasizes that studies in the science of morals must be based on disciplined observation, impartiality, a framework for determining what to observe, and systematic research techniques used consistently and self-consciously.[1] Observers of human society must follow the precepts of the natural philosopher: avoid prejudgment and hasty generalization, sample widely, gather the facts, and recognize that some facts are more valuable than others (ibid., 17–19).

The original intention of the book was to provide "for travellers and students" necessary instruction regarding the "inquiry or observation into social manners." The terms 'morals' and 'manners' in the nineteenth-century context referred to values, cultural standards for behavior, and the 'character' of a society, on the one hand, and patterns of human interaction or 'social intercourse' on the other, rather like the distinction between culture (mores or norms) and social behavior (folkways). In her interest in the "theory and practice of society," Martineau wished to explore and expose the relation between social institutions, values, and behavior. As she demonstrates in her America books, she identified the internal criteria for understanding and assessing a society. But this required knowledge of principles of research and appropriate training.

> The powers of observation must be trained, and habits of method in arranging the materials presented to the eye must be acquired before the student possesses the requisites for understanding what he contemplates . . . The observer of Men and Manners stands as much in need of intellectual preparation as any other student . . . Every man seems to imagine that he can understand men at a glance; he supposes that it is enough to be among them to know that they are doing; he thinks that eyes, ears, and memory are enough for morals, though they would not qualify him for botanical or statistical observation . . . the science [of Morals], of all the sciences which have yet opened upon men, is perhaps, the least cultivated, the least definite, the least ascertained in itself, and the most difficult in its application (*How To* . . . , 1–3).

How To Observe Morals and Manners covers three topics: "Requisites for Observation," "What To Observe," and "Mechanical Methods." Contrary to the book's title, it devotes far more space to *what* one should observe in a society – the social institutions and culture – than to the philosophical foundations of social investigation or the methods and techniques for carrying it out. Nonetheless, even the discussion of what to observe reflects Martineau's strong historical and comparative view, as she integrates a considerable amount of description and analysis in the book, which reflected, by the time of its publication in 1838, the results of her study of America.

51

Martineau insists on two principles of sociological understanding, natural law, and cause and effect:

> His [the observer's] first general principle is, that the law of nature is the only one by which mankind at large can be judged. His second must be, that every prevalent virtue or vice is the result of the particular circumstances amid which the society exists (ibid., 33).

She discusses the moral requisites for observation which include especially a capacity for sympathy and openness to others, and freedom from prejudice in one's attempt to understand a people and their rules for conduct.

Martineau's practicality and astuteness about working in the "field" are apparent in her discussions of methods and techniques for doing research. In the gathering of facts she advocates: (1) the use of different modes of transportation to give one exposure to a variety of perspectives and people; (2) a thorough knowledge of the language; (3) techniques for the corroboration of facts and observations – research tools such as a diary, to record one's personal reactions; a journal, to record impressions, incidents, anecdotes, descriptions; and a notebook, to record the facts of daily life.

In her discussion of "what to observe" Martineau presents her macrosociological framework, as we would call it now, for studying a total society, of which, she notes, there are too few examples. One must begin the "inquiry into morals and manners with the study of THINGS, using the DISCOURSE OF PERSONS as a commentary upon them" (ibid., 63). Facts must be gained from the "records" of a society:

> architectural remains, epitaphs, civic registers, national music, or any other of the thousand manifestations of the common mind which may be found among every people (ibid.).

The institutional areas which must be examined include: religion, general moral notions (national character, popular culture, literature, the treatment of criminals), the domestic state (geography, economics and occupation, family, class, health), the idea of liberty (law, servitude, communications, education, opinion), progress (cultural, economic, and technological change), and discourse (values, interests, and goals of a society). Martineau's discussions of each of these areas reflect her ability to see the interrelations of institutions and of behavior and moral norms. Like Montesquieu, she wants to consider the totality of society, including its geographical, climatic and economic bases. Like Condorcet, she considers the truest test of a civilization to be the freedom and equality accorded to women. Like Marx, she examines the class structure and its consequences in religion, the family, education, politics, and liberty. Like Durkheim, she considers the morals, values, and religion of a society to be the foundation of its sociological integrity.

It is ironic that this book, now so important to our understanding of Harriet Martineau as the "first woman sociologist," was given far less attention by her and her readership than almost any of her writings. It was not reprinted and was virtually lost for a century and a half. Within the historical emergence of the moral sciences and, specifically, of sociology, *How To Observe Morals and Manners* takes its place as the first methodological treatise in the field.[2]

Harriet Martineau arrived in New York on 19 September 1834. Before sailing on the return trip to England on 1 August 1836, she spent nearly two years travelling close to 10,000 miles throughout the United States, visiting many areas more than once, talking with and interviewing people of all ages, classes, races, religions, and political parties. She was entertained by the President of the United States, Andrew Jackson, and she conversed with slaves in the cotton fields. She spent considerable time with James Madison, Henry Clay, William Lloyd Garrison, William Channing, Ralph Waldo Emerson, Dr. Charles Follen, Maria Weston Chapman, as well as with Supreme Court justices and members of Congress. She talked with mill girls, Indian tribes, members of experimental communities, abolitionists, and feminists. She visited prisons, hospitals, mental asylums, literary and scientific institutions, factories, plantations and farms, and lived in all sorts of dwellings from stately homes to log houses. She used wagons and stagecoaches, trains, horses, barges and boats, and her own feet as means of transportation. Martineau was always an early riser and a great walker. She often arose to watch the sunrise as it illuminated the landscape, as on the Hudson River, or to watch the fisherman go out to sea, as during her stay in Gloucester, Massachusetts. She found natural wonders and occurrences to treasure in every locale she visited. Her descriptive accounts of her travels in America of the 1830s make pleasurable reading if only for her observations and commentaries on exciting vistas, the variety of plant and animal life, wild flowers, and birds. Her itinerary included all regions of the United States with longest visits in New England in particular and the Northeast in general.[3]

Martineau's deafness by then made her quite dependent on an ear trumpet, "a trumpet of remarkable fidelity," which provided an interesting entrée for her conversations with people. Recognizing the need for assistance in gleaning information, impressions, and exchanges, and for another set of ears, Martineau brought with her a congenial, intelligent and suitable companion, Louisa Jeffrey, who had volunteered to accompany her in return for expenses minus the cost of passage (Webb 1959, 139–40).

The lengthy American visit was not an easy one. The two women suffered many inconveniences and often lived in difficult or even dangerous circumstances. Unlike the usual portrayal of Martineau as demanding, intolerant, and rigid, she was an enquiring, adventuresome, and tolerant traveller, perseverant in the face of social and physical difficulties.

Like all Europeans, Martineau was fascinated with the American experiment in politics and government, and she sought to understand their workings and to convey the system's advantages and disadvantages. She understood the variety of state governments to be due to differences in climate, history, customs, and prejudices. She was concerned about the strength of individualism in American society, which could contribute to the detriment of the community (*Society in America* 1:40). And she recognized that much of the intolerance and mob behavior of the day was perpetrated by middle-class "gentlemen" (*SA,* 1:163–64). She became acutely aware of the strong sectional prejudices which exuded hatred not seen even in the worst times of English-American conflict. But she was optimistic about America, particularly when compared in certain respects with England. She saw the economy and the expanding division of labor as offering great opportunities; education as more accessible for all children; property and marriage laws as more equitable for women; natural resources in abundance and natural beauty as gifts for all. She was enthusiastic about the country's possibilities truly to realize the ideals of the Enlightenment. Nevertheless, the situation of slavery and the subordinate status of women hung like black clouds over this New World paradise. In fact, Martineau witnessed a great deal of turmoil and pain in American life in this pre-Civil War period.

There were many aspects of her tour which were pearls in the crown of life experience. In more than one hotel or cabin she saw "the stars through the chinks in our walls," and once slept in a room where the lower half of the window was missing, as a deer had leaped through it a few weeks before (ibid., 231–32). Martineau enjoyed the adventure in West Virginia of climbing up to a rocky ledge called the Hawks' Nest overlooking the Kanawha River twelve hundred feet below and of exploring miles of the Mammouth Cave in Kentucky. She took a lesson in rifle shooting, hitting within an inch at twenty-five paces, but "thought it best to leave off with credit" (ibid., 271). In Kentucky also she enjoyed a view of the last herd of wild buffalo in that area, and witnessed, perhaps too closely, the ritual of felling and burning a bee-tree: "I returned, stung, but having seen what I wanted . . . it was impossible to help laughing" (ibid., 274). She fell off a log trying to cross a stream and roared with laughter as she stood in water up to her waist. She donned the appropriate dress and walked the ledges behind Niagara Falls. She was not to miss an adventure if she could help it!

Martineau was fascinated by American Indians and observed their particular ways: women carrying large baskets on their backs and walking barefoot while their "lords" rode before them. She noted that the Negroes preferred to be the slaves of Indians instead of the whites for they received kinder treatment. She sympathized with the plight of the Indians against the claims of squatters.

Martineau found enlightened women in the South who taught their slaves how to run an estate. But the absence of sound priorities led her to lament the American emphasis on money rather than on education and literacy. Harriet was proud of her ability to adjust ("I generally acted as a pioneer"), particularly in the frontier situations of the midwest. She took particular notice of the flowers everywhere and of the wild strawberries of (Tecumseh) Michigan, so delicious that even the local children would not sell them. "Money is no object for them." I began to think that we had got to the end of the world; or rather, perhaps, to the beginning of another and better" (ibid., 327).

Martineau had strong opinions. She disliked the Shakers' "spiritual pride, insane vanity, and intellectual torpor," and their obsession with celibacy. She was strongly critical of slaveholders who wished to expand their territories to fortify slavery and assure the power of the slave states in Congress. She had little sympathy for Americans' complaints about the immigration of foreigners (their greatest complaint) who had provided the labor for most of the public projects and agriculture. Martineau thought that immigration, in fact, had helped the moral life of the society. She had harsh criticism for the manners and affectations of the wealthy American, which she saw as deviations from the republican spirit. She concluded that many of the foibles of American society reflected its mercenary tone.

Slavery was of course the greatest economic and political anomaly, and Martineau found sound economic arguments against it, which she outlined in her analysis of slavery and capital and the relation of land, labor and population in America. She saw the political future of the South to be increasingly dismal if slavery continued.

Martineau tried to expose herself to every aspect of life in America. She visited patients in asylums, convicts in prison, the Quadroon women in New Orleans. She interviewed men in solitary confinement. As one who appreciated the positive aspects of being left alone, in her subsequent books on America she pointed out the advantages of that confinement, as well as the plights of the prisoners.

Martineau's investigation of America resulted in two, three-volume studies, the first of which was *Society in America* published in 1837. Her original title, *Theory and Practice of Society in America*, which better expressed her purpose, was rejected by the publishers Saunders and Otley. Martineau's study of American society is part of a tradition of such investigations by predecessors such as Montesquieu, contemporaries such as Tocqueville and the Trollopes, and successors in the twentieth century such as Gunnar Myrdal. Like them, Martineau examined the society and its institutions, compared them with European societies and exposed the discrepancies between the cultural values and norms of American society and that society's actual behavior or practice. Her purpose was clear from the beginning: "to compare the existing state of society in America with the principles on which it was professedly founded; thus testing Institutions, Morals and Manners by an indisputable, instead of an arbitrary standard, and securing to myself the same point of view with my readers of both nations" (ibid., vii). In addition she proposed "to enable my readers to judge for themselves, better than I can for them, what my testimony is worth" (ibid., ix) by giving an account of her itinerary complete with dates and the means employed to obtain her information.[4]

She responded to the objections that being a woman with previously known views posed disadvantages for her by emphasizing the increased access she enjoyed as a woman to the private locales of American life – "the nursery, the boudoir, the kitchen, all excellent schools in which to learn the morals and manners of a people" as well as the access she had as an accomplished public figure to public and professional affairs. Indeed, she viewed her single disadvantage as her deafness, for which she compensated by use of her assistant Louisa Jeffrey and, of course, her ear trumpet.

Society in America is among the most thorough sociological studies of a society in the nineteenth century. Martineau investigated government and politics, all sectors of the economy and the social institutions, 'Civilization' as she called them. She described the structure or 'apparatus' of each institution and then analyzed the actual functioning or operation of these structures, particularly in terms of the values and principles which were being articulated. Her investigation was descriptive, analytical, and critical.

In examining government and politics, Martineau stressed the strengths of the system – its principles – and the potential for genuine democracy. "Politics are morals, all the world over; that is, politics universally implicate the duty and happiness of man" (*SA*, 1,6). It is in the arena of politics, a lifelong interest of Martineau, that the theory and practice of a nation's principles intersect, where material realities and the highest ideals confront one another. The theory that "the majority are in the right" requires that basic principles be secured and that the citizenry have the liberty to ensure a correspondence between the principles and their institutional forms. The inconsistencies arose out of human fallibility rather than political design. She placed great hope in the power of the majority if wisely and tolerantly used, in the relation between the federal and state governments if cooperatively conducted, in the productive and commercial capacities if based upon free labor and fair practices, and in the openness of the public forum if resistant to the tyranny of public opinion. The shortfalls were a function of an immature sense of freedom and responsibility, and of selfish individualism which neglected social duty and human benevolence.

In discussing the party system Martineau notes the vagueness of antagonism between the two political parties in America, probably due to the absence of an old aristocracy. Differences among classes in knowledge and wealth are compensated by a desire of all for law and order and pursuit of personal goals. But even in these early discussions, Martineau recognizes that the contradictions of the oppression of negroes and the "political nonexistence" of women defy the political realization of the nation's principles. She explores the structures and practices of the federal and state governments, the exigencies of political life in America, newspapers, civic apathy, and regional prejudice, and the legal and political exclusions of negroes and women.

> It is an absorbing thing to watch the process of world-making;
> – both the formation of the natural and the conventional
> world. I witnessed both in America. (*SA*, 210).

The natural world unfolded before Martineau's eyes – in the depths of Mammoth Cave, Kentucky, behind the roar of the falls at Niagara, on the waters of the Mississippi. "The primitive glories of nature" prepared the possibilities for the realization of the conventional world; for Martineau, advancement and progress were everywhere. In studying the economy she takes account of the immense natural wealth and the variety of inhabitants, major factors in the development of this nation. She examines the economies of agriculture, transport and markets, manufactures, and commerce, mostly in descriptive terms, as they were being shaped in various regions of the country. The delicate relationship between the Federal and state governments and business and industry are considered, particularly with regard to currency and commerce. In discussing government expenditures she announces the salaries of the country's leading officials – $25,000 for President Jackson, $5,000 for the Vice-President, $6,000 for the Secretaries of State and the Post-master-General, among others – and the numbers maintained for defense.

Society in America is far less factual than Martineau's later similar analyses; she was still very much the traveller and enjoyed describing the impressive variety of sites and people. But she was particularly concerned with the moral life of the society, and so she ends this part of her account with significant chapters on the morals of the economy: slavery, manufactures and commerce. Her discussions of relations among the white settlers, the native inhabitants, slaves, new immigrants, and women are anecdotal but nonetheless sociological, as she shows how power operates in human relationships, how the morality of society is sustained by its practices, how newspapers reinforce ignorance and injustice, how women, slaves, and immigrants are exploited.

In the third volume of *Society in America* Martineau examines "civilization," which in the old world still corresponded with the low idea that "the generality of men live for wealth, ease and dignity and lofty reputation" rather than for inner values. Although the new world was forged out of the principles of truth and justice – the grounds for revolutionary struggle and for the Declaration of Independence – its members remained captivated by the old world's pursuit of wealth rather than social and political freedoms. Her greatest concern about American society, apart from its denial of justice to slaves and women, was its mercenary character. Indeed, the dissatisfactions of the moralists, the scholars, the professionals, and even the merchants with life in America had to do with the importance of, and demands attached to, the pursuit of wealth over other values.

In the ensuing chapters Martineau discusses the values and relations among social classes and identifies Americans' style as generous and friendly, with a desire to communicate on a variety of subjects. Then she explores the status of women and children and "sufferers," those who are marginalized by virtue of being criminal, mentally ill, handicapped, poor, or alcoholic. She was particularly interested in the ways in which society responded to the needs of sufferers, and again concluded that it did so with considerable generosity, perhaps by comparison with England. In a chapter on "Utterance" she discusses

America's rather unsatisfactory literary life. Its representatives like Cooper, Bryant, and Bancroft have been less than successful by English standards, she thought. From Martineau's perspective, Americans had benefited more from the writings of Carlyle, Wordsworth, Anna Jameson, and Hannah More.

The final segment of *Society in America* concerns religion, and here Martineau exercized her sociological skills with considerable finesse. A general discussion of the practice of religion in daily life reveals the presence of intolerance of infidelity, regional misunderstandings, and pressure to conform to religious norms. She laments the "dreadful infringement on human rights throughout the north" regarding religious opinion and "how little chance Christianity has in consequence of this infringement" (*SA*, 3:238). Martineau distinguishes the science of religion from its spirit and practice and, in separate chapters, expounds on the study of the history, theology, and current status of religion, the spiritual ethic and meaning of religion, and the "administration," or what we would call the social organization, of religion in America. The challenge for the new nation is to make it possible for its members to live their lives according to their own convictions.

As a young author Martineau had studied and written about religion on many occasions. So it is not surprising that Part IV of *Society in America* is devoted entirely to the subject. She was struck by the lack of diversity in religious beliefs in a country which exalted freedom of conscience. And she noted many instances of religious intolerance, anti-Catholicism, persecution of atheists, and violation of Christian principles. Indeed, she was quite critical of the clergy itself for ignoring "the grand truths of religion, or principles of morals," particularly mutual justice, charity, and liberty in regards to slavery. She cited several examples of the collusion of the clergy with the practices of the slave system and the religious justification of it. At the very least, their fear of controversy made the clergy ineffective. There were instances, she recognized, in which churches served as vehicles for compassion and justice, for example, the efforts of the churches of Boston in the abolition of slavery. A plea for strengthening theology in America was based upon her conviction at that time that religion is "the root of all democracy; the highest fact in the Rights of Man."

In exploring the spirit of religion Martineau was more optimistic. She saw the possibility for its full development among the members of society to be great, as indicated by acts of Christian charity, religious curiosity, and asceticism. In Martineau's view puritanism was a significant aspect of American religious life.

Martineau concludes that, while her observations must necessarily be tentative, American society has a smaller amount of crime, poverty, and mutual injury of every kind than any known society. "They have realised many things for which the rest of the world is still struggling" (*SA*, 3, 298). They are self-governing and have avoided an aristocracy, a link between church and state, and excessive taxation. The "tremendous anomaly" which must be cast out is slavery. But she is required to conclude that "the civilisation and the morals of the Americans fall far below their own principles" (ibid., 299).

Martineau did not hesitate to deal with controversial issues in her research in America and in her subsequent reports. This new nation, lacking a feudal tradition and based upon Enlightenment ideals, was formed of self-governing, self-reliant rugged individuals who, in the process of surviving the wilderness and building a nation, produced a country of open market competition combined with a persistent sense of social status. Martineau observed that this nation of 'equals' created its own new kind of hierarchy and class distinctions which illustrated the 'tenacity of rank' in society. The ideal of equality, upon which the Republic was founded, confronted such contradictions as the dependent status of women, their 'political nonexistence', and the institution of slavery. Martineau discussed the similarities in the two cases of oppression; the nation of equals was, in reality, a polity of white privileged males.

The situation in America, according to Martineau, was compounded by apathy among the citizens and timidity of the press. A press which shunned its responsibilities only added to the paralysis of the principles upon which a republic is based. "The exercise of the suffrage is the first duty of republican citizenship" (ibid., 157), and those who enjoy the privilege in America do not use it. She was almost as dismayed by the lack of political participation (only 10–12 percent of the population voted) as by its denial to women and blacks. She discovered that the frequent disregard for the law and the taking of the law into one's own hands was a phenomenon of the American middle classes, the "gentlemen", who ignored the government and its laws which they alone had created.

Martineau's strongest analysis regarding human rights and human relations in the new society appeared in Part III "Civilization." Looking for national character, she felt that it was too soon to expect this in the new republic, but certain traits were already apparent: arrogance in the South, timidity in the North and comfortable self-complacency in the West. Particularly impressive to her was the great influence of public opinion in American society, dangerous for the people and the culture.

Women in America

In one of the most forceful and poignant critiques on the status of women in the nineteenth century, Martineau analyzed the "Political Nonexistence of Women," a chapter which surely stirred controversy among its readers.

> Governments in the United States have power to tax women who hold property; to divorce them from their husbands; to fine, imprison, and execute them for certain offenses. Whence do these governments derive their powers? They are not 'just,' as they are not derived from the consent of the women thus governed.
>
> Governments in the United States have power to enslave certain women; and also to punish other women for inhuman treatment of such slaves. Neither of these powers are 'just;' not being derived from the consent of the governed.
>
> Governments decree to women in some States half their husbands' property; in others one-third. In some, a woman, on her marriage, is made to yield all her property to her husband; in others, to retain a portion, or the whole, in her own hands. Whence do governments derive the unjust power of thus disposing of property without the consent of the governed (ibid., 199–200)?

In a democratic society these practices were wrong, but the fundamental question of women's rights had been evaded. Martineau did not limit the issue to America:

62

The question has been asked, from time to time, in more countries than one, how obedience to the laws can be required of women, when no woman has, either actually or virtually, given any assent to any law. No plausible answer has . . . been offered; for the good reason, that no plausible answer can be devised. The most principled democratic writers on government have on this subject sunk into fallacies (ibid.).

In strong and convincing passages, Martineau criticized Jefferson in America and James Mill in England for their views that men must protect women's purity by their exclusion from the political sphere and that women's interests are best represented by their husbands and fathers (ibid., 201–2). She argued that women's interests are not identical with those of men, cannot be represented by them and are capably and validly put forward only by women themselves. The status of women and slaves in American society could only be lamented.

If a test of civilization be sought, none can be so sure as the condition of that half of society over which the other half has power, – from the exercise of the right of the strongest . . . The Americans have, in the treatment of women, fallen below, not only their own democratic principles, but the practice of some parts of the Old World . . . While woman's intellect in confined, her morals crushed, her health ruined, her weaknesses encouraged, and her strength punished, she is told that her lot is cast in the paradise of women: and there is no country in the world where there is so much boasting of the 'chivalrous' treatment she enjoys (SA, 3:105–6).

Martineau pointed out that the education of women in America was similar to that in England; women were taught those things which fill up their time and make them good companions to their husbands. Women who tried to excel in professions such as education were shunned, particularly those women who declared their anti-slavery opinions. Religion, the sole base of knowledge for women, was in the circumstances only a vehicle for women's oppression, providing the rationale and norms for their subordinate state. And the assumption that there were male and female virtues created a self-fulfilling prophecy.

By contrast, Martineau thought that marriage and divorce

laws in America were a great improvement over England and offered considerable advantages to women, particularly regarding the rights of property in some states. However, too often marriage was an instrument of expediency: young girls married too soon, and young women married old men. Martineau insisted that the "victims" themselves must take responsibility for change:

> I have no sympathy for those who, under any pressure of circumstances, sacrifice their heart's-love for legal prostitution . . . . and least of all could I sympathise with women who set the example of marrying for an establishment in a new country (ibid., 128).

For Martineau the most serious problem for American women was the lack of occupation. Women were not allowed any vocation outside marriage and domestic life, and they were poorly trained even for that. The absence of fundamental household skills and reliance on domestic servants increased women's dependencies and further lowered their condition. The ultimate problem for many women was lack of opportunity to earn their own bread. And the female labor which did exist received scanty rewards. Certainly, Martineau understood that equality for women and elimination of their subservience depended on economic self-reliance.

The health of American women was the final link in the chain of their submission. Lack of exercise and fresh air and a generally poor diet debilitated women. Idleness and a "vacuity of mind" generated vices and intemperance in the use of spirits which became "hereditary," she observed.

The fate of children, like that of women, was *potentially* superior in America because of the availability of free education to the general population, at least in the North. However, although children had more freedom in America than in England, they were encouraged to yield to authority rather than to learn self-sufficiency.

In this *Lettres persanes* genre the author was reflecting upon the British context as well as upon her own utilitarian background. We see that it was not simply a matter of what was "useful" or "expedient" for the prosperity and progress of a nation, but a question of conducting societal affairs according to its proclaimed principles and values and according to the natural laws of human society.

> However the Americans may fall short, in practice, of the professed principles of their association, they have realized many things for which the rest of the civilized world is still struggling. They are, to all intents and purposes, self-governed ... They have one anomaly to cast out; a deadly sin against their own principles to abjure. But they are doing this with an earnestness which proves the national heart is sound (*SA*, 3:298).

Her major conclusion was that "the civilisation and the morals of the Americans fall far below their own principles" (ibid., 300).

Slavery in America

> I was a well-known anti-slavery writer before I thought of going to America; and my desire to see the operation of the system of Slavery could hardly be wrongly interpreted by any one who took an interest in my proceedings (*Auto.*, 2:17).

Harriet Martineau had always been an abolitionist. It was part of the Unitarian tradition and of her education. As early as 1830, in a review of two articles in the *Edinburgh Review* and the *Westminster Review* and in another review in the *Monthly Repository*, she condemned slavery as contrary to Christianity and unacceptable in the colonies of England.

> Every man in every country feels that it can never be right to torture women, to condemn men to exile and toil, to separate children from their mothers, to subject the helpless to the violence of the strong, to make life one scene of hardship, pain, and degradation ("West India Slavery," *MR*, iv:5).

In 1832 she took up the issue of slavery in *Demerara*, one of her political economy tales. Martineau explained in the preface that her portrayal of the negroes in the story was intended to show them as they were, real human beings, and to show their claims against slavery. *Demerara* was widely read and praised in England and gave Martineau a reputation as a strong abolitionist.

Consequently, even in the first few months of her visit in America, she was warned by friend and foe alike not to travel in the South, and she was often attacked in the press.

In her writings Martineau maintained that the most fundamental problem with slavery was its dismissal of the principles of human rights or natural right, the philosophic basis of the new republic. The basic assumption in the slave system was always that blacks were incapable of managing freedom and therefore needed the protection and supervision of whites. In her chapter on "The Morals of Slavery" in *Society in America* Martineau explained how the white gentry actually preserved its own oppression by laws which, meant to maintain the system and control blacks, actually restricted the freedom of movement and thought of their makers. No amount of mercy, patience, and benevolence on the part of the slave owners could justify that system. Whites paid the price in poor schools, few and poor quality newspapers, and the constant unease and fear of blacks as potential threats to themselves and their families.

In *Retrospect of Western Travel,* the three-volume, ethnographic report on her American trip which followed *Society in America* and was written especially for her English audience, Martineau described some of her early impressions and experiences with the slavery issue.[5] She commented that in Baltimore the bodies of negroes were taken for dissection "because whites do not like it and the coloured people cannot resist." It was ironic, she observed, that though the body is assumed to be analogous with a white and all the parts are "nicely investigated" for scientific knowledge, medical men came from such a study with contempt, hatred, and insult.

Martineau was drawn into the abolitionist scene in November 1834 in Philadelphia, "the city of brotherly love," when confronted by an acquaintance who wanted to know whether she would prevent, if she could, the marriage of a white person with a person of color. When she replied that she would never try to interfere with persons who loved each other, this "eminent religionist" screamed in horror, "then you are an Amalgamationist!" Although by the time Martineau travelled through the South her views on the subject became well known, she experienced neither insult nor danger while visiting the southern states.

In August 1835 Martineau attended a meeting of the Ladies'

Anti-Slavery Society at the Boston home of Francis Jackson at the time when public opinion in Boston was vehemently anti-abolitionist. During the meeting of 130 women and a few men, Ellis Grey Loring asked Martineau whether she would "give a word of sympathy to those who are suffering here for what you have advocated elsewhere" (*Auto.*, 2:30). Martineau did not wish to jeopardize her remaining travel and investigation. "I should no more see persons and things as they ordinarily were . . . and my very life would be, like other people's, endangered [but] I felt that I could never be happy again if I refused what was asked of me" (ibid.). At that moment she felt no choice but to say a few words to the abolitionists.

> I had supposed that my presence here would be understood as showing my sympathy with you . . . I will say what I have said through the whole South, in every family where I have been; that I consider Slavery as inconsistent with the law of God, and as incompatible with the course of his Providence. I should certainly say no less at the North than at the South concerning this utter abomination – and I now declare that in your *principles* I fully agree (ibid., 2:31).

The consequences of simply stating her principled position were remarkable. It must be remembered that, although Martineau had been against slavery from early on, she initially felt that the tactics of the American abolitionists worked against the cause (Webb 1960, 151–56). Maria Chapman and William Lloyd Garrison were important in convincing her, by the spring of 1836, of the efficacy of the abolition movement. Soon after her Boston remarks, Martineau felt the repercussions in letters and in newspapers in the North and South. Her life was threatened by many, particularly Southerners, with the consequence that she did not make a second trip to the Southern states as originally planned.

Martineau continued to write about slavery in America and the abolitionist movement after her return to England. In "The Martyr Age of the United States" in the *London and Westminster Review* for December 1838, she reviewed the Annual Reports of the Female Anti-Slavery Society of 1835, 1836, and 1837. "Slavery is as thoroughly interwoven with American institutions as the aristocratic spirit pervades Great Britain" (*LWR*, 22:2).[6]

She observed that the Colonization Society, originally considered even by Garrison to be a positive scheme for the enslaved, turned out to be a tactic for disposing of "useless" or problem slaves and for assuring the continuation of the slave trade. The conversion of Garrison to abolitionism and and the long tale of heroic acts on the part of abolitionists portrayed real struggles. She wrote about the persecution and prosecution of Prudence Crandall for establishing a school for "young Ladies and little Misses of Colour"; she discussed the role of the antislavery associations, institutions such as Oberlin Institute (College), Lane Seminary in Cincinnati, and heroes such as Amos Dresser (a Lane student who was prosecuted for carrying abolitionist literature), Maria Weston Chapman, the Grimkes, Lydia Child, Lucretia Mott, E.P. Lovejoy, and John Quincy Adams in their struggles against slavery in various places, particularly in the District of Columbia. She showed the corruption of American principles of free speech and freedom of movement with such attempted censures as the Gag Bill.

Martineau chose to emphasize passages from these annual reports which illustrated the connections between the enslavement of Blacks and the subordination of women. For example, the General Conventions of Women in 1837 and 1838 in America were regarded as threats to the authority of the male clergy who soundly condemned the women for their outrageous and obstreperous behavior. Soon, people like Dr. Follen and Adams were defending the rights of women and the Ladies' Anti-Slavery Societies against such groups as the General Association of Massachusetts Clergymen, who maintained that women should not discuss such matters without their pastors' consent.

In "A History of the American Compromises," which appeared in the *Daily News* and was subsequently reprinted as a book in 1856, Martineau focused on the politics of slavery as regards statehood, and the political power of the slave-holding minority. In "The Manifest Destiny of the American Union" which appeared in the *Westminster Review* of July 1857, Martineau, reviewing three publications dealing with the slavery issue plus her own 1856 publication, focused on the political consequences of slavery in the form of states' rights and the increase of violence among whites as well as between blacks and whites. She described the responses in the South to the threat of abolition, which included censorship, the kidnapping of northern white children for slavery, threats to withdraw southern students from northern universities, and a pervasive paranoia and suspicion, particularly of women.

> Various Southern papers call upon the citizens to keep a vigilant eye on all female strangers, who appear as schoolmistresses, governesses, lecturers, or travellers, as 'the Southern States are rustling with the petticoats of emissaries sent by the Abolitionists' (*WR* 1857, 171).

The "second revolution," the withdrawal of states from the Union to save the institution of slavery, was encouraged by the facts that the abolitionists remained outside the political and military spheres and that the will of the North was not as strong as that of the South, according to Martineau. The situation was further complicated by the overrepresentation of Southern sympathizers on the federal Supreme Court. She asserted that the constitutional problems, if not quickly resolved, would lead to the dissolution of the Union, but hoped that the abolitionists would persevere in upholding the democratic principles upon which the country was founded.

In an article entitled "The Slave Trade in 1858" (*ER* 1858, 276–99), Martineau reviewed the American slaveholders' journal, *The London Cotton Plant*. She seemed convinced then that slavery as a practice was on the way to extinction and that the desperate claims of American slaveholders indicated the death gasp of the slave system. Martineau wrote a number of essays and reviews on the conflict, concluding in 1864 in the *Edinburgh Review* that secession, meant to preserve slavery, was the very act which hastened the emancipation and the inevitable demise of the inhuman system. The issue of slavery was indeed a lifelong concern for her.

The years 1836 to 1838, following her return to England, were busy and varied for Harriet Martineau. She completed the writing of her America books and her methodology treatise at the encouragement, if not pleading, of several publishers. The British wished to hear all they could about America, and Martineau's perspective was keenly sought. She eventually accepted Saunders and Otley's proposal of £900 plus twenty-five copies for *Society in America* and later £600 plus copies of *Retrospect of Western Travel*. The promise to her of all proceeds from the sale of her books in America, over and above expenses, was never kept.

Martineau was somewhat ambivalent about her first book on America, reflecting in her *Autobiography* that it was too theoretical in its "metaphysical framework." This was also one of the strengths of the book, in that it revealed a sociological theory or perspective in her work. Nevertheless, letters from both sides of the Atlantic showed that she had aroused her readers to the issues and had expanded her sympathetic public. There were, of course, reactions of rage from pro-slavery Americans and from those who objected to Martineau's forthrightness in her criticisms of American society. She had no regrets in spite of the "metaphysical" bent of *Society in America* and "never regretted its boldness of speech."

A few years after her return from America an incident of considerable significance to Martineau occurred. In America a little slave girl, Ailsie, who had been a subject in Martineau's *Retrospect of Western Travel*, was in difficulty due to the death of her mistress. The latter's Irish widower, unreconciled to the institution of slavery, felt unable to protect Ailsie, a mulatto child of a negro cook and a white slave owner, from the abuse of the cook's husband as well as from whites who despised mulattoes. Upon his wife's death he wrote to Martineau to ask if she could take the girl, to which she responded positively. Her plan was to keep the girl in her Ambleside home, send her to school and then ascertain "what she was most fit for." After preparation and months of waiting, she received word that the girl was gone, back to the ownership of the dead woman's mother, who had presented Ailsie to her daughter as a wedding gift. The fate of the young mulatto who "in her ripening beauty was too valuable to be given to me" haunted Harriet. "For what purposes she was detained . . . there is no need to describe. She was already lost and gone; and I have never heard of her since" (*Auto.*, 2:144).

The America books strengthened Martineau's reputation as a leading social analyst and generated new opportunities for her. In December 1837 the firm of Saunders and Otley, publishers of her books on America, asked her to become editor of a proposed new periodical "to treat of philosophical principles, abstract and applied, of sociology."[7] The terms were very suitable, giving her an opportunity to become financially secure and to work on a subject about which she felt confident. Irresolution and worry about the responsibility were accompanied by a realization of the great opportunity at hand. Her diary recorded the agony:

> It is an awful choice before me! Such facilities for usefulness and activity of knowledge; such certain toil and bondage; such risk of failure and descent from my position! The realities of life press upon me now. If I do this, I must brace myself up to do and suffer like a man. No more waywardness, precipitation, and reliance on allowance from others! Undertaking a man's duty, I must brave a man's fate. I must be prudent, independent, serene, good-humored; earnest with cheerfulness. The possibility is open before me of showing what a periodical with a perfect temper may be: – also, of setting women forward at once into the rank of men of business. But the hazards are great, I wonder how it will end (*Auto.*, 2:110).

Although her friends encouraged her to do it, her brother James, whose opinion counted for more than anyone else's, was absolutely against it. Harriet had been vacillating over the matter, but, as soon as she received James's advice by letter, she declined the offer. While it is true that she was now free to pursue numerous other avenues, including writing a novel, this was a significant and perhaps unfortunate decision. The offered position would have taken her much more directly into economics and sociology and would no doubt have expanded her contacts with contemporaries working on similar social and economic issues. In spite of the missed opportunity, her interest in, and perspectives on, social and economic questions continued to grow.

In the remarkable *How To Observe Morals and Manners*, Martineau had displayed an understanding of social research, as seen in her explications on methodology. In the following year, 1839, she wrote her *Guide To Service* series which, while containing practical directions for prospective employees, yields many insights into the sociology of these occupations. Her article on "Domestic Service" in England in the *Westminster Review* in August 1838 is a fascinating essay on the social and psychological aspects of domestic service, replete with insights on

71

social classes and class relations in England at the time. Exposing especially the lot of the "maid of all work" and criticising English women's attitudes towards servants, she developed, through a comparison of domestic relations in America and England, the argument that master and servant relations must be changed and improved for the good of society.

Perhaps most interesting in this essay are Martineau's arguments about the importance and meaning of work. The servant is doing his (sic) duty and should not be disdained; those who live lives of idleness, economically comfortable women particularly, should regard this as a curse not a privilege. She called for "the self-education of the employing class – the study of the philosophy of Work, and the cultivation of sympathy of human feelings" as a means of rectifying the position of one party and dispelling the prejudices and tempering the feelings of the other ("Domestic Service," *LWR* August 1838, 432).

There are certain contradictions in the writings of Harriet Martineau; for example, she expresses a belief in middle-class virtues and then argues on behalf of the working classes and the oppressed in society. Like Saint-Simon, she welcomed the increasingly specialized division of labor in industrial society and asserted that all tasks were to be respected. Every social class had an interest in making the system work smoothly. Unlike some of her conservative contemporaries she was concerned that people should be treated fairly and rights recognized.

After several years of addressing herself to the principles of society and economy and to social issues and social problems, Martineau longed to get away from pure fact-finding and the constraints of 'objective' analysis. She wanted to write fiction. And she began to plan a novel. She also developed an idea for an historical romance.

A novel portraying the lives of middle-class Victorians grew from a story, told to Martineau by a friend, about a man who was forced by a matchmaker into an unhappy marriage to the sister of the woman whom he truly loved. He was told that the sister had fallen in love with him, having misinterpreted the attention he had shown her, and he felt morally bound to go through with the marriage for the sake of her honor and feelings. The story captivated Martineau, and she contrived characters and a setting in which to tell the story in her novel *Deer-*

brook, published in 1838. Unsure as she was about writing a novel, she found it a relief "to many pent up sufferings, feelings and convictions." Novels about the middle classes were still unusual:

> People liked high life in novels, and low life, and ancient life: and any rank presented by Dickens . . . but it was not supposed that they would bear a presentment of the familiar life of every day (*Auto.*, 2:115).

Deerbrook was published by Moxon in three volumes and two editions, and Martineau was amused "to hear the daughters of dissenting ministers and manufacturers expressing disgust that the heroine came from Birmingham, and that the hero was a surgeon" (ibid.). As Robert Webb points out, it was an important book precisely because of its middle-class context, its character as a "woman's book," and its portrayal of the idea "to stand for principle and to suffer for it" embodied in Edward Hope, a physician and the protagonist. One significant theme of the novel is the link between truth and science and the ultimate triumph of science over ignorance and superstition.[8]

A second significance of the novel centers on Martineau's treatment of the occupation of governess, portrayed in the life and character of Maria Young.[9] The occupation is one of sacrifice, dependence, and marginality. Maria is alone, hardworking and unlikely to marry. At that time the occupations of governess and doctor had much in common: both worked in private homes as professionals but were considered social inferiors to their employer-patients, in spite of surpassing them in education (Saunders 1986, 72).

Her novel showed the influence of Jane Austen and reflected, in many respects, Martineau's philosophy and view of the world of ideas at that time. This was a period in which her impending break with religion, increasing interest in science, and growing economic security as a woman were beginning to coalesce. The virtues of duty and perseverance embodied in the lives of her characters were those so consciously upheld by the author herself. Martineau wished to emphasize the thought and actions of her characters and to show the folly of allowing sentiment, emotion, and weakness of character to dominate human lives.[10]

Perhaps less emphasized but equally important in the book is its community setting and the examination of the lives of individuals, constituting a web of social relations in which each person has complicated and far-reaching effects on others. The consequences of class position, occupation, marital status, and gender for one's place and credibility in the community are well portrayed. The implications of social values and norms for the lives of individuals were well drawn, as Martineau showed the pressures toward marriage for women and toward occupational success and respectability for men. She used characters who in important ways overcame or rejected the limitations of early Victorian standards. The novel addressed itself particularly to the question of the choices for women in this context. However qualified its status among the great novels of the nineteenth century, *Deerbrook* provides an excellent picture of middle-class life and social relations. It had considerable impact on its readership, including George Eliot and Charlotte Brontë who were inspired by it in their own writing.

As these projects and others, including the *Guide to Service* series and articles for current periodicals, were being conducted and new works being planned, Martineau's writings were becoming increasingly popular among the British and American publics. Her many endeavors and strict work schedule were beginning to exact a price, however, and though she said little of it, by the summer of 1837 she felt somewhat weakened in physical strength and was in a depressed psychological state. She had the responsibility of her mother and aunt, who were experiencing the increasing effects of old age. Work had become a refuge. But in 1839 illness overpowered her.

The accession of Queen Victoria in 1837 was an important even for Martineau, who had been made aware that the young Victoria was reading her political economy series with great enthusiasm. Martineau's account of the Coronation on 28 June 1838 is interesting and amusing. A delightful description of the grandeur of the occasion begins with her remark that dressing "in crape (sic), blonde and pearls" at four in the morning seemed very strange. Having arrived at the Abbey early, she found the long wait for the ceremony tedious, and she settled into her book and sandwich, leaning against a pillar to ease her fatigue (*Auto.*, 2:118–29). Later, having trouble seeing and hearing, she stood on the rail behind her seat, while holding on to another rail. Exhausted but having enjoyed the day, she reflected on the occasion:

It strengthened, instead of relaxing my sense of the unreal character of monarchy in England. The contrast between the traditional ascription of power to the sovereign and the actual fact was too strong to be overpowered by pageantry, music, and the blasphemous religious services of the day. After all was said and sung, the sovereign remained a nominal ruler, who could not govern by her own mind and will; who had influence, but no political power; a throne and crown, but with the knowledge of everybody that the virtue had gone out of them. The festival was a highly barbaric one, to my eyes (*Auto.*, 2:127).

Notes

1. Read in conjunction with her two major expositions on America, *Society in America* (1837) and *Retrospect of Western Travel* (1838), *How To Observe Morals and Manners* (1838) reveals the intent and context of these studies and helps us to understand their organization and insights. It is reminiscent of Montesquieu and parallels the work of Tocqueville, as do all her America books. The book went relatively unnoticed during Martineau's life and is one of only two of her books not published beyond a first edition. Its significance for the history of sociological research is only now being recognized. The book was reprinted by Transaction Publishers in 1989.
2. It is superseded possibly only by Saint-Simon's *Introduction to the Scientific Studies of the 19th Century* (1808) and *Essay on the Science of Man* (1813), which she undoubtedly read in the early 1830s. The methodological discussions of Auguste Comte were published in segments from 1830 to 1842, but it is unlikely that Martineau had studied those of 1830 and 1835 in detail, or at all, before she finished and published her own treatise in 1838. The influence of Montesquieu, Locke, and Condorcet can be seen in this work as well as in her America books.
3. Martineau provides a general itinerary in her introduction to *Society in America*. A more detailed compilation of dates, places, and prominent persons visited is given by William R. Seat, Jr. (*Notes and Queries*, June 1959, 6:207–8). She visited New York City, Albany, Schenectady, Utica, Buffalo, Niagara Falls, Northumberland and Philadelphia, Pa., Baltimore, Washington, D.C., Mount

Vernon and Charlottesville, Va., Columbia and Charleston, S.C., Augusta and Columbus, Ga., Montgomery and Mobile, Ala., New Orleans, Nashville, Mammouth Cave and Lexington, Ky., Cincinnati, Sulphur Springs and Charleston, West Va., West Point, Stockbridge, Northampton, Boston, Cambridge, Deerfield, Salem, Cape Ann and Plymouth, Mass., Saratoga Springs, Glenn Falls and Lake George, N.Y., Detroit, southern Michigan (Niles, Tecumseh, Ypsilanti, Ann Arbor), Michigan City and La Porte, Ind., Chicago, Milwaukee, Mackinac Island, Cleveland, Beaver, Pittsburgh and Economy, Pa. Martineau tells of the concern of the ship's captain, upon their arrival in New York, as to whether she had anti-slavery opinions and had professed them in public. New York newspapers contained reports of her impending arrival, and before Martineau was allowed to disembark, the captain had to be assured that she had said more than once during the voyage that she came to learn, not to teach (*Auto.*, 2:11).

4. She begins her study clearly aware of the limitations of one individual's perspective in conducting such an investigation, and so cautions to her readers. She seems remarkably modest and open to scrutiny while confident that she has been as thorough as possible under the circumstances. "In working according to this method, my principal dangers are two. I am in danger of not fully apprehending the principles on which society in the United States is founded; and of erring in the application to these of the facts which came under my notice. In the last respect, I am utterly hopeless of my own accuracy. It is in the highest degree improbably that my scanty gleanings in the wide field of American society should present a precisely fair sample of the whole. I can only explain that I have spared no pains to discover the truth, in both divisions of my task; and invite correction, in all errors of fact. This I earnestly do; holding myself, of course, an equal judge with others in matters of opinion" (*SA*, 1: viii).

5. *Retrospect of Western Travel* contains chapters on a variety of experiences, impressions, and interpretations of American life directed particularly toward Martineau's British audience – chapters discuss important individuals such as Priestley, Channing, Madison, and Colonel Burr; cities such as Washington, New Orleans, and Cincinnati; regions of the country which were particularly impressive; and social institutions ranging from Harvard Commencement to slave market fairs to cemeteries.

6. Martineau pointed out that slaveholders constituted only 350,000 out of a nation of 27,000,000 and that representation in the House was based on a count which included the slave population. She analyzed with clarity and insight the Fugitive Slave Law, which required free states to turn over fugitive slaves to their respective slave states, and the politics of territory and the pressure to expand slavery. The issue came down to the question, as Charles Sumner put it, "whether Liberty shall be sectional and Slavery national, or the reverse."

7. Transcript of letters of Harriet to James Martineau, Dec. 12 and 21, 1837, Manchester College Library, Oxford.
8. Webb 1960, 183–89.
9. For an excellent discussion of Martineau's Maria, see Sanders 1986, 59–71.
10. See Sander's analysis.

4   Controversial Afflictions

Thou seekest Health; and how?
Let gloom and tears no more thy spirit bow;
Health springs aloft upon the viewless wind:
Up to the mountain top pursue her flight;
Over the fresh turf track her footsteps light,
In hawthorn bowers, 'mid fountains gushing bright,
      Seek her, and thou shalt find.
               —"Consolations," 1830

Reason is on your side, and nature too: –
Nature, who bade the human soul be free,
Active and independent, gave it power
To seek the truth and energy to hold.
   The mind of man must keep its onward course,
And conquer prejudice and combat error,
Till truth prevail, clear, gentle, and serene.
      — from "Address to the Avowed Arians of
           the Synod of Ulster," 1830

In the fall of 1838 Harriet took a journey, accompanied by friends, to Newcastle, the Lake District, and Scotland. In Newcastle she attended a meeting of the British Association for the Advancement of Science, at which there were only "two or three valuable addresses" and where she was ashamed of the disinterested and trivial behavior of the women who attended. The trip to the Lake District fostered her interest in that area where, in less than a decade, she would build her permanent home. She revisited Scotland (where she and James had hiked in their youth) with a view to exploring the topography for Mr. Knight for a forthcoming edition of Shakespeare's plays. She intended to do the same for the Italian plays in a trip to Italy.

In April 1839 Martineau left for a trip on the Continent with three other women travellers and a maid-servant. While walking in Germany she seemed on the verge of illness, and by the time of the party's arrival in Venice, she was very ill, and it became evident that she would have to return to England. She was brought by carriage to the Rhine, where she was met by her brothers and brother-in-law and taken back to Fludyer Street in London. Her illness incapacitated her for the next five years.

Martineau's physician was her brother-in-law, Thomas M. Greenhow, husband of her sister Elizabeth. Since they lived in Newcastle-upon-Tyne, Harriet was taken there, first to a house in their neighborhood, then for six months with the family. She longed for solitude and did not wish to impose on the household, so she moved a short distance away to Tynemouth, where she took two rooms with a lovely view of the sea in the house of a Mrs. Halliday. There, with a young companion Jane, and a maid who kept her quarters spotless, Harriet spent the years 1839–44 as an invalid.

Life in the Sickroom

From the time of her teens Harriet had suffered, in addition to deafness, from episodes of low physical strength, various aches and pains, and consequent low spirits. She had been under considerable physical and mental stress since her publishing career began. Her mother had nursed her in earlier periods, but now her mother was going blind, and her elderly aunt required full care. Worrying about them added to Martineau's anxiety; this, in turn, contributed to the deteriorating state of her health by 1838–39.

Martineau's illness became a controversial affliction on several counts. She had gynecological problems, namely, a prolapsed uterus and an ovarian cyst. The uterus was enlarged and crowded other organs, causing secondary problems, such as pain in other areas, particularly the back, and rather severe menstrual problems. The treatment prescribed consisted of leeches, opiates, rest, and iodide of iron. Martineau was convinced that her illness was "unquestionably the result of excessive anxiety of mind, – of the extreme tension of nerves under which I had been living for some years, while the three anxious members of my family were, I may say, on my hands" (*Auto.*, 2:150).

Although she was confined to a sofa for nearly six years, she was "comparatively happy in my release from responsibility, anxiety, and suspense." No real improvement occurred for some time, but she was by no means totally disabled. In fact, she was able to work and, like many other Victorian invalids including Darwin, Eliot, and Browning, took full advantage of her new situation to do so. During the next six years she wrote a number of books, some of which related to her illness. In addition to writing, she received many friends and counselled and corresponded with politicians, businessmen, and intellectuals on the affairs of the day.

Her first project was an historical novel, a tribute to Toussaint L'Ouverture. A Haitian who led his people in revolt against French rule, he had been Martineau's hero for some time. She had written an account of his life for *Penny Magazine* in 1838, partly as a message to both blacks and whites in the American South as to "what a negro has been, and what other negroes may be" (Arbuckle, 11). On her continental trip she visited his grave in France and made the decision to write a novel about his life. She began *The Hour and the Man* in early May and by mid-November was correcting proofs; the novel was published early in 1841. Inspired both by Wordsworth's poem about him and by historical reports, she portrayed the black hero in an exaggerated, larger-than-life fashion. The novel was another expression of her support for black emancipation. Although the review in the *Athenaeum* (1840) implored her to keep negroes out of "our imaginative literature," the novel received high praise from Florence Nightingale, Maria Edgeworth, Thomas Carlyle ("as beautiful as a child's heart") and American abolitionists such as Maria Chapman and Wendell Phillips. It went through several editions.[1]

In spite of her illness she began another writing project almost immediately. This was "light and easy work," a series of children's stories to be entitled *The Playfellow*. Such an entertaining enterprise would have obvious appeal for her under the circumstances, but it is likely that she wrote them with the income in mind. These stories, of quite distinct settings and contexts, were intended to both entertain and teach children, and to transmit a moral about good spirit and right conduct. They remained extremely popular among children well into the twentieth century.

Contrary to the rather whimsical title, the stories concerned the physical and spiritual survival of children under adversity. Located in a variety of settings, the four stories – *Settlers at Home, The Peasant and The Prince, Feats on the Fiord,* and *The Crofton Boys*

– represented a new approach in children's literature; realism and drama replaced the more reserved motifs traditionally found. The books were very successful, particularly *Feats on the Fiord*, which was reprinted in many editions, and *The Crofton Boys*, which George Eliot thought "exquisite."[2]

Martineau's Study of Illness

During those years as an invalid confined to her rooms overlooking the sea in Tynemouth, Martineau "accumulated a weight of ideas and experiences which [she] longed to utter" regarding her illness and confinement. In September of 1843 she began to write a volume of "essays from the sickroom." She claimed that she never wrote anything so fast – "It went off like sleep . . . so strong was the need to speak." Although *Life in the Sickroom* was published anonymously in 1844, her authorship was readily detected.[3] The book had a lengthy dedication to an unnamed friend, probably Elizabeth Barrett Browning, also an invalid at the time. The two corresponded and shared a mutual admiration for each other's work.

The book is an interesting sociological analysis of illness, from the perspective of the patient as well as of those in attendance. A considerable portion of the book concerns itself with a plea to the invalid to avoid being a burden on her caretakers and instructions to the latter to be honest and direct in talk with and care of the sick. Although the book may be a "self-righteous little volume [which] breathed a self-conscious air of noble suffering," as Pichanik comments, it reflects Martineau's understanding of the social aspects of illness.[4] She analyzes the special position of the patient who has, by virtue of being somewhat out of daily life, a more detached view and an ability to put things into perspective. Martineau reflected considerably in the book on the progress of history and the evolution of society.

By 1844, as Martineau's condition did not appear to improve, several of her friends, including her brother James and Bulwer-Lytton, suggested that she try mesmerism. Feeling rather desperate, in pain, and convinced that she was bound for lifelong invalidism, Harriet decided to try mesmeric treatment. Mesmerism, or animal-magnetism, was based on the idea that the presence of magnetic fluid in human beings (who are subject to the principles of electricity and magnetism which operate in the world at large) allowed certain individuals to magnetize others, relieve pain and induce sleep or somnambulism. The practice of mesmerism was used in the treatment or healing of physical and mental problems and by 1843 was called "hypnosis" (Pichanick, 130).

In June 1844 Martineau was visited by the mesmerist Spencer Hall, who, by the passing of hands, was able almost immediately to give her some relief from her pain and discomfort. She was given continuing mesmeric treatments by Hall and a Mrs. Wynyard, and by her companion Jane, who had learned to mesmerize during this period. Jane even mesmerized Martineau's nightclothes to beneficial effect! Martineau's pain decreased, allowing her to give up the opiates upon which she had become too dependent.[5]

From that time on Martineau's health improved rapidly. She became convinced that the mesmerism had reduced the tumor to a harmless state. As her pain lessened, she gained more energy. By the autumn of 1844 she was able to enjoy her walks out-of-doors once again. By January 1845 she and Jane were ready to leave Tynemouth to visit family and settle into lodgings near Windermere.

By contrast, Dr Greenhow attributed Martineau's improvements in appetite, energy, and general physical and psychological health to the iodide of iron remedy. According to him, Martineau had been making the expected progress over a period of years. But Harriet was convinced that it was mesmerism which brought about her recovery. Consistent with her constant urge to communicate new information to the public, Martineau wrote about her experience in a series of "Letters on Mesmerism" published in the *Athenaeum* in several installments and then as a single volume by Moxon in 1845.

Martineau's use of such a controversial cure, her challenge to medicine, to religious thinking, and to middle-class propriety, caused a furor and created considerable public debate. Many of her friends publicly and privately decried her advocacy of mesmerism, although it should be remembered that many Victorians made use of mesmerism for various illnesses. Adding to the controversy was the publication by her brother-in-law of the facts of Harriet's case with little attempt to keep the patient's identification anonymous. He had asked her permission to publish the case in a medical journal and, so Harriet assumed, in Latin for professional readers. Instead, he published his account in a shilling pamphlet in English, clearly intended for public consumption, with the title *Medical Report of The Case of Miss H—— M——*. Greenhow clearly was attempting to protect his medical reputation by discrediting the effects of her mesmeric treatments. All the data were there – the status of Harriet's uterus, how it responded to examination, description of the discharges, and, of course, his assertion that she had been recovering under medical treatment, that mesmerism had nothing to do with the changes. In fact, Greenhow had had serious doubts earlier about the likelihood of recovery. Harriet was clearly upset by the incident and particularly angered by Greenhow's false assertion that he had the patient's permission to publish the account as it appeared.

Her family's reaction was mixed; her mother and sisters were concerned about the medical reputation of Greenhow and were convinced that the mesmeric "cure" would damage Harriet's public image. Because of the controversy Mrs. Martineau, for a time, avoided seeing Harriet, who reflected years later "from that time forward they [her mother and sister] were never again to me what they had been" (*Auto.*, 2:172). But as she had "the sympathy of all the world — even the medical profession" by now, Martineau did not pursue the Greenhow matter further. Indeed, criticism from religious and medical ranks was countered to a great extent by interest in her successful "treatment" and support from friends and doctors, some of whom sent patients to her and her mesmerist.

The entire experience of prolonged illness and mesmeric cure had major significance for Martineau's life and thought. It demonstrated to her the validity of phrenology and the unity of mind and body. It showed the interrelation of being, feeling, and thinking, and the effects on each of animal-magnetism. It was most of all a successful empirical experiment; the results were tangible. Now she understood cause and effect in a new way. Having developed over the years her doubts about religion, she was unafraid of the gossip and warnings about the blasphemy or unnaturalness of mesmerism. And having experienced and witnessed clear, concrete results, she was drawn closer to phrenology and to an increasing reliance on the empirical and the practical. It all seemed to converge into a clarified whole for her after she met and collaborated with the individual who was soon to replace James as the most important male figure in her life, Henry George Atkinson.

The Scientific Paradigm–Letters on the Laws of Man's Nature and Development

Harriet Martineau first heard of Henry George Atkinson in 1844 in a letter from Mr. and Mrs. Basil Montague, who encouraged her to try mesmeric treatments. They referred to Atkinson as a successful mesmerist and "our dear young friend" (*Auto.*, 2:192). Although Martineau and Atkinson actually met in May 1845, he had advised her from mid-1844, via mutual friends, on mesmeric treatments. He had also helped her to engage Mrs. Wynyard as a mesmerist. From her *Autobiography* it is clear that from their first meeting Martineau was utterly captivated by Atkinson. A cultured and charming man (*Auto.*, 2:213–19), he was interested in science, experimentation, and the exchange of ideas, was moderately educated and travelled, and lived off his inheritance. But it was not until after her trip to the Middle East in 1846 and the writing of *Eastern Life: Past and Present* (Chapter Five) that Harriet began to explore Atkinson's philosophical views. That book reveals how far Martineau had moved in her views on religion, by then seeing it as a social institution influenced by changes within the larger society.

Martineau's collaboration with Atkinson, which she initiated and which culminated in the publication in 1851 of *The Letters on the Laws of Man's Nature and Development*, grew out of her recognition of a compatibility of their ideas and perspectives. Her ideas on science, religion, causation, and truth had evolved over a long period. She had moved from being a Unitarian theist to a rationalist and positivist agnostic. Atkinson became important to her precisely because he subscribed to similar ideas regarding mesmerism, phrenology and science. This provided her with support and confirmation of her views and reassurance that she was not alone.

The Martineau-Atkinson friendship was one of strong attraction and mutual respect. The relationship is a rather fascinating one: a young man committed to an enduring friendship with a woman ten years his senior, who was possibly even more devoted to him; a collaboration for a book in which ideas are exchanged and explored between a man and a woman, unusual in Victorian England or perhaps anywhere; and the relationship itself, one of commitment if not sexuality, loyalty if not romance.[6] Although Martineau's description of "first seeing Mr Atkinson" has the air of the first encounter with one's beloved, the terms of their enduring friendship were set early when Martineau suggested that they exchange letters, lightly offering her promise not to fall in love with him. Neither Martineau or Atkinson doubted that their first encounter, in 1845, was a "meeting of minds." But Martineau admitted that, perhaps because of her own personality and her deafness, her tendency to talk too much, and her weaker background in philosophy, it was years before she learned to know Atkinson (*Auto.*, 2:216).

The experience of mesmerism had convinced Martineau of the importance of inherent forces in human existence and of natural laws which directed the course of social and natural occurrences. One had to understand one's place among these forces and to see life as the pursuit of harmony with them. Martineau returned to necessarian philosophy and the writings of Hartley, Bacon, and others. As she understood her own thinking at the time, she needed to replace "the hopelessness of the metaphysical point of view, and its uncertain method and infinite diversity of conclusions," with the positive method, "and its uniform and reliable conclusions" (*Auto.*, 2:217); she used her "dialogues" with Atkinson to work through the problem. Because their collaboration provided another instance of controversy around Martineau, the relationship and the resulting book are included in this chapter. We will take, therefore, a temporary leap in time to the early 1850s.

The purpose of *The Letters on the Laws of Man's Nature and Development* was to instruct others on universal natural laws and the relation of man to the physical and natural world through Baconian method. It was meant as an elucidation of positive philosophy (positive science). While Atkinson defined philosophy as "the observation of effects in relation to causes, in order [to lead] to the discovery of the laws concerned" (*LLMN*, 20), those who read the book were less concerned about positive philosophy than about the authors' agnosticism and naturalism. A few years after publication Martineau wrote:

It is a curious fact that, of all the multitude of adverse reviews of our book that we read, there was not one that took the least notice of its essential part, – its philosophical Method (*Auto.*, 2:218).

Apart from Martineau's intellectually subordinate posture and exaggerated portrayal of Atkinson's astuteness in the book, their collaboration was a means for Martineau to clarify and to make public her convictions about natural and positive philosophy as the foundation of her belief system.[7] Her increasing faith in science as the basis of modern society and, indeed, of philosophy itself, and her firmly established skepticism about religion were affirmed in her discussions with Atkinson. She felt she wanted to share it all with the world. While Martineau's passionate commitment to science as the basis of progress and of happy improved lives for members of society was widely shared among active thinkers and writers of her generation, her daring to put forward radical rationalist ideas directly and uncompromisingly caused an uproar. Martineau was less certain of herself in the areas of phrenology and mesmerism, and for that depended on Atkinson. Most of the ideas in the book are expressed by Atkinson in letters to her – the master teaching the student; she had allowed him to be her voice.[8]

What were the basic ideas presented by Atkinson and Martineau? Following Joseph Priestley and the doctrine of necessity, they stressed the unity of Nature, human beings as a part of Nature subject to natural law and therefore to the principles of cause and effect, the link of mind and body, the materiality of human beings – Enlightenment ideas prevalent in intellectual and scientific circles and best summarized by the doctrines of necessarianism and materialism. Their perspective, like that of Priestley, emphasized that humans were "voluntary agents" who made choices in a context shaped neither by Calvinist determination nor the complete freedom of philosophical liberty, but by an imperative toward the perfection of oneself and others.[9] Like many of their scientific contemporaries, they approached the science of human nature through phrenology, which assumed that the human mind and therefore human behavior were functions of the physiological structure of the brain.[10] By examination of the skull's shape and protuberances, the character of an individual could be predicted. Franz Gall had paved the way with his dissections of the brain, but Martineau and Atkinson saw the limitations of his method and the need for other approaches. Mesmerism seemed to offer the most promising possibilities for understanding of the mind-body relationship. This quasi-scientific approach incorporated the power of intuition or clairvoyance, and thus seemed to integrate the rational-scientific with the intuitive-spiritual philosophies of knowing.[11] The whole question of the will was an element in the initial impetus for Martineau and Atkinson's "studies." Free will had to be discounted in the face of inherent and determinant natural laws to which all of nature, human beings included, were subject.

The reception of a Martineau book is always fascinating. The reviews and reactions were mixed, often contradictory and ambivalent, reflecting the character of the "Victorian frame of mind." The readers of *Letters on the Laws of Man's Nature and Development* were shocked, offended, hurt, encouraged, forgiving, insulted, dismayed, accepting.[12] And the reactions were often quite unexpected.

Charlotte Brontë, who at first warned Harriet that the book would bring her "troublous times," later wrote: "You are tender of others: – you are serious, reverent and gentle. Who can be angry?" Her response meant a great deal to Martineau, because Charlotte

> admitted and accepted my explanation that I was an atheist in the vulgar sense, – that of rejecting the popular theology, – but not in the philosophical sense, of denying a First Cause . . . She saw that truth and Man would never advance if they must wait for the weak (*Auto.*, 2:351).

Elizabeth Gaskell has shown that Brontë had a sympathetic and affectionate opinion of Martineau and respected her for her "consistency, benevolence, and perseverance" (Gaskell, 328). However the *Letters*. . . . truly distressed Brontë, who wrote to publisher George Smith: "It is the first avowed atheism and materialism I have ever read; the first unequivocal declaration of disbelief in the existence of a God or a future life I have ever seen" (ibid., 329). But Gaskell emphasizes that Brontë "could not bear the contemptuous tone in which this work was spoken of by critics; it made her more indignant than almost any other circumstance during my acquaintance with her" (ibid, 330).

Although George Eliot, like many others, apparently was surprised if not shocked by the alleged atheism of the two, she was very interested in the social theories of her generation and encouraged Martineau in her project to translate Comte. She declared that Harriet Martineau "is a trump – the only English woman that possesses thoroughly the art of writing" (Haight, 2:32). Eliot visited Martineau and retained her friendship until Martineau withdrew because of Eliot's relationship with George Lewes. Eliot never reversed her admiring attitude and wanted to be among the first to write a venerating obituary of Martineau upon her death, then anticipated in the late 1850s.

The debate over the book had to do considerably with the issue of materialism, but for Martineau and Atkinson the point which was misunderstood or ignored was that the spiritual and the material are interrelated in the context of experienced reality. Their curious and rather disorganized book was an attempt to show that interconnection, not to herald an idealist or materialist perspective but to show the unity of nature and of experience.[13] As Postlethwaite has summarized it:

> Like Charles Bray, Atkinson and Martineau found in the combination of phrenology with mesmerism what they considered the perfect synthesis: a science that is also a religion; an empirical explanation for the realm of intuitive truths; the union of positivist law with phenomena beyond the ordinary powers of the senses (Postlethwaite, 153).

In her *Autobiography* Martineau recalled the words of Martin Luther: "If your faith is worth anything, it does not depend on me: and if it depends on me, it is not worth anything" (*Auto.*, 2:352), commenting that she was surprised at how little faith some had, including those who called themselves "freethinkers." She felt that those of confirmed orthodox beliefs in fact treated the book and its authors far better than the "heretical" reformers. It was a test of her relationships as well. "This book has been an inestimable blessing to me by dissolving all false relations and confirming all true ones" (ibid., 357). Just as the pleasures of climbing the Great Pyramid could not obliterate the "fatigue and awfulness of it," so the pain and misunderstanding resulting from the "Atkinson Letters," as she called them, could not be underrated or forgotten.

Atkinson was criticized for having published with a woman and was advised to "do himself justice" and publish alone, while Martineau was criticized for "lending my literary experience to any man's objects" (ibid., 360). (Of course, the presentation of the ideas as part of a discourse with a male colleague undoubtedly contributed, or so Martineau anticipated, to more serious consideration in an era when women were not accepted as part of the *avant garde*.) As might be expected, one author was played off against the other, depending on the views of the reviewer. But the greatest problem was the focus of reviewers on the theology rather than the philosophy and science in the book. Although the book shows a rather superficial understanding of science, the authors' primary purpose was to convey to the general reader their enthusiasm for a science of human nature; it was Martineau's attempt to convince the educated middle classes of the importance of pursuing the science of human nature for the sake of knowledge and of practical everyday life.

The relief that Harriet must have felt in pronouncing to the world once and for all her beliefs about the natural and supernatural was quickly jarred by the judgment of the one person whose opinion could affect her most profoundly – her brother James, then an editor for the *Prospective Review*. James not only volunteered to review the book but insisted upon doing so in spite of the reservations of his fellow editors. The review was a devastating, at times nasty, condemnation of the book and its authors. Without warning or advance discussion, James publicly aired his views of Harriet and her collaborator; he even suggested that she should feel ashamed for having subordinated herself to such an intellectual charlatan. It was, of course, the book's apparent atheism which was most objectionable to him.[14]

The event was the climax in the long-deteriorating relationship between Harriet and James. He had become increasingly skeptical of her intellectual course since her endorsement and use of mesmerism in the early 1840s. And he was no doubt upset at the relativism and historical radicalism expressed in 1848 in her *Eastern Life*, in which Harriet suggests that all Western religions derived from that of ancient Egypt and where she views religion as a social and historical rather than revelational phenomenon. Perhaps even more important was the fact that Harriet had become a well-known figure in British society, consulted, visited, and written to by politicians, intellectuals, and scientists. It seems quite clear, particularly in light of James's persistently negative and discouraging attitude to all of Martineau's new adventures and opportunities, that he was jealous of his sister's success and public stature.

Martineau withstood the controversy over her use of mesmerism and her alleged atheism. She was strong and did not doubt that the outcry would pass. She was not prepared, however, for public condemnation by her brother; the pain and unhappiness generated by the event were to last the rest of her life.

Notes

1. Wheatley, 218–219. Martineau broke with literary tradition again, as she had with *Deerbrook*, in writing a novel featuring a black hero. Dr. Channing wrote: "You have given a magnificent picture, and I know not where the heroic character is more grandly conceived" (*Auto.*, 3:241).

2. *The Crofton Boys* is about life in a boys' school, where protagonist Hugh Proctor, whose foot is amputated following an accident, must overcome consequent physical and psychological difficulties, including having a hard and rather cruel mother. He overcomes adversity and becomes a successful adult.

   A particularly interesting analysis of the story by Diana Postlethwaite suggests that Agnes, Hugh's sister, who tends to her needlework, cares for her brother after the accident, and longingly watches as he goes out into the world, first to school and then to India, is in many ways Martineau herself. The story seems to express the author's anger about the separate and dominant male world and her anxiety over her own suffering and loss of hearing and of health in general (Postlethwaite, "Mothering and Mesmerism in the Life of Harriet Martineau," *Signs*, 14:583–609).

3. Included in this reflection on the thoughts and experiences of the invalid were a number of her convictions. In particular, she discussed the importance of and attraction to biography as a means to understanding history. The pursuit of the truth of people's lives, however, could not sacrifice their privacy. She stated firmly that public exposure of one's private correspondence is unacceptable and that she had taken steps to prevent it from happening in her case. Martineau did, in fact, ask her correspondents to destroy her letters, and she destroyed those she received which went beyond business matters.

4. Pichanick 1980, 128.

5. Mesmerism, the forerunner of hypnotism, was a controversial treatment. Its principle was the relief of pain and illness through the transmission of magnetic influence.

6. Among the many commentators on their relationship, Robert Webb, Martineau's best-known biographer, maintains that the relationship was defined by the likelihood that Atkinson was homosexual and spent most of his time engaged in liaisons in Europe, and that Martineau was either utterly celibate or, more likely, a lesbian who would not have become involved romantically with Atkinson. His suspicion is raised by her pattern of living with several women in her household. Carroll Smith-Rosenberg maintains that historians have been extremely influenced by Freudian theory in their analyses of same-sex relationships, seeing them as the root of childhood deviance, trauma in adolescence, detecting "the symptoms of 'latent' homosexuality in the lives of both those who later became 'overtly' homosexual and those who did not" (Smith-Rosenberg 1985, 53). She argues that women's relationships with one another were characterized by closeness, free emotional expression and uninhibited physical contact, unlike male-female relationships in the nineteenth century which seemed more consistent with women's socialization. (ibid., 74). Martineau made it quite clear that her dedication to her work left no time for romantic involvement with men, although she had several close male friends.

7. The roots of her positivism, as has been shown, lay in her early education with its Unitarian orientation towards science and rationalism. Martineau had searched then almost desperately for theological and philosophical answers which could be of practical and meditative value to her. Positivism, built on the idea of the unity of the sciences, explored the laws of nature at all levels of reality. The science of the mind, which Comte called *la morale* and of which phrenology was a part, was the logical outgrowth of the science of society, sociology, which had emerged from biology in the hierarchy of the sciences, according to Comte. As Postlethwaite and others have suggested, mesmerism and phrenology furnished Martineau and other devotees with explanations and relief from physical suffering not provided by other sources, such as religion.

8. See Postlethwaite's enlightening book, *Making It Whole*, especially Chapter Three, "New Faiths . . . ," 110–63.

9. See James J. Hoecker's *Joseph Priestley and The Idea of Progress*, 1987, especially Chapter Two, "Necessity, Matter and Mechanism." David Hartley's theory of associationism, a sensationist, reductionist theory of the mind, was combined with phrenology, mesmerism, and intuitionism in the Martineau-Atkinson exchanges. Materialism, which emphasized the importance of the concrete material aspects of human experience, provided a progressive response to the "ideological" and irrational theories and practices emanating from philosophical idealism and operative Christianity (Hoecker, 70).

10. The interest in phrenology was, in fact, quite widespread in England during the first half of the nineteenth century, following visiting lectures by Johann Spurzheim, a colleague of Franz Gall. It had captured the interests of many important British intellectuals who were part of the "turn-of-the-century" generation, the leading figure of the movement being George Combe (1791–1855). Phrenological societies, journals, books, and lectures had appeared in abundance. The "science" of phrenology was seen as a means of understanding human behavior from an empirical perspective and of demonstrating the link between physiology and behavior. (Parssinen, 1974).

11. The rather inconsistent and contradictory elements found in *The Letters* ... resulted from trying to come to terms with the rational and the irrational elements operating in the relation between mind and body, thought and behavior, as Postlethwaite suggests.

12. See Pichanick and Postlethwaite for good discussions of reactions to *Letters*.

13. See Chapter 22 of *Letters*. Martineau and Atkinson tried to make it clear that they were setting aside the question of First Cause and were concentrating on the material world of experience. However, they were critical of "gross materialism" which ignores "the obscure imponderable agents, and the study of vital action and the real powers of Nature" (*LLMN*, 274).

14. James Martineau, "Mesmeric Atheism," *Prospective Review*, 7:224–62. James later became an important figure in the Unitarian church, in higher education, and in English life and letters.

5 The Historian and Social Scientist

Hail to the steadfast soul
Which unflinching and keen
Wrought to erase from its depth
Mist and illusion and fear!
Hail to the spirit which dared
Trust its own thought, before yet
Echoed her back by the crowd!
Hail to the courage which gave
Voice to its creed, ere the creed
Won consecration from time!
—Matthew Arnold for Harriet Martineau,
"Haworth Churchyard," 1852

The 1840s was an eventful decade for Harriet Martineau. By 1844 she had recovered sufficiently from her illness, or at least from its symptoms, to resume the rigorous work schedule which she normally placed on herself. While ill she had longed for the Lake District and as soon as possible took lodgings there, but after considering the inadequacies of her rented quarters at Waterhead on Lake Windermere and her desire to live permanently in the area, she purchased for £95 a two-acre field with a small, rocky hill near Ambleside and had a house built there during the winter of 1845–46. She planned and oversaw the construction of her new home, which she appropriately named The Knoll and finally occupied in April 1846. A two-story structure of dark gray Westmoreland stone, its imposing structure contained bay windows, gables, and numerous chimneys, and housed a drawing room, a magnificent study, and library. An impressive staircase led to her own quarters and rooms which accommodated many friends over the following years. The home was filled with gifts of art, furniture, writing accoutrements, and personal tokens of various sorts given to Martineau by her many friends. The surrounding garden contained an astounding variety of flowers, shrubs, and trees, including the stone-pine planted by Wordsworth and two oaks planted by Macready. A granite sundial given by a friend in London still stands in place. It contains her own motto, approved by Wordsworth, her elderly neighbor at nearby Rydal Mount: "Come, Light! visit me!"

The library at The Knoll consisted of three thousand books. Art, biography, education, literature, geography, travel, history, morals and politics, political economy, theology, and works of reference particularly government documents of all sorts, dictionaries, reports of commissions, and publications on all subjects of concern to government were well represented. Unusual for the times was the extensive collection on women's duties and rights (*Auto.*, 3:261–87).

Upon the completion of her own house, she had a cottage built below the hill for her farm man and wife, as well as several outbuildings, including a pig house and a cow stable. The occupants of the two-acre farm produced most of their food. Part of Martineau's joy in small farming came from the meager entrepreneurial gain from surplus milk sold to neighbors. Always fond of children, she looked forward to the daily visits from her young neighbors, who came to buy milk.

Her knowledge of and enthusiasm for managing the farm were conveyed in "Our Farm of Two Acres," which appeared originally in *Once A Week* magazine and later in the volume on *Health, Husbandry and Handicraft* (1861) and in an 1865 pamphlet. The three-part essay demonstrated how hard work and organization allowed this household of women and one farm man to provide for their own needs and support while living (at least on Martineau's part!) a balanced existence of the soothing pleasures of rural life and the active life of the mind.

Life in Ambleside suited Harriet. She could preserve her privacy by avoiding the lionizing and frenetic social life of London and the persistent socializing of a small town so as to have time for writing and reflection. But she left Ambleside during the summer to escape curious tourists and to visit London and other locales. Nevertheless, some of her renowned neighbors became part of her social network in Ambleside. The Wordsworths advised her from the beginning regarding the purchase of the Knoll, and the aging William planted a tree in Harriet's garden. She was close friends with Thomas and Matthew Arnold, but perhaps she felt greatest kinship with Mary Wordsworth and Mary Arnold and other women in the community (Webb, 258). In addition to pleasant neighbors, Martineau's social circle included friends who visited her at the Knoll over the years, such as Henry Crabb Robinson, Charlotte Brontë, George Eliot, Henry Atkinson, Erasmus Darwin, William Rathbone Greg and James Payn.

Establishing her residence in Ambleside did not mean in any way that Martineau was extricating herself from politics and current issues. As a fund-raiser for the Anti-Corn Law League, Martineau published *Dawn Island, A Tale* in 1845, the proceeds of which went entirely to aiding the League. Martineau had long campaigned against the Corn Laws and this was a substantial contribution on her part toward the cause of repeal. *The Forest and Game Law Tales* of 1845 were written at the request of John Bright, whose Committee on the Game Laws wished to draw public attention to the privileges of old gaming laws which were detrimental to the farmers and especially to the poor. Webb points out that both undertakings were related to the anti-corn law agitation and the general issues of free trade. Although nearly 2,000 copies of the tales were sold, the sales were not in the usual range for Martineau books and were considered in those terms a failure (Webb 1960, 266).

Eastern Life

In the autumn of 1846 Martineau was invited by Richard V. Yates and his wife to accompany them on a trip to the Middle East. She was encouraged by everyone to go, and although she had just embarked on a new series of *The Playfellow* with the tale *The Billow and The Rock*, she made arrangements for care of the house and for Jane, her maid and mesmerizer from her days in Tynemouth who had come to live with her in Ambleside, and prepared for the journey.

The seven-month trip through the Middle East – Egypt, Sinai, Palestine, and Syria – was a fascinating adventure. In many respects the ruggedness and strangeness of the journey appealed to Martineau. She was determined to absorb as much as possible in those exotic settings. Her travelling companions (who included the Yateses and Mr. Joseph C. Ewart, and was to have included Atkinson) enjoyed considerable compatibility, which was enhanced by their practice of spending large parts of each day independently. This left Martineau needed time for quiet meditation about her experiences and the book she wanted to write about them:

All the historical hints I had gained from my school days onward now rose up amidst a wholly new light. It is impossible for even erudite home-stayers to conceive what is gained by seeing for one's self the scenes of history, after any considerable preparation of philosophical thought (*Auto.*, 2:278).

The book, *Eastern Life: Past and Present*, was extraordinary in several respects. It was a travelogue, part of a large collection of travel books of that period written by British and French middle-class men and women, who for numerous reasons swarmed over the globe. It was an historical-archaeological account of the monuments, temples, and natural and cultural life of the region. Specifically, it considered the origins and the historical relativity of Judaism, Christianity, and Islam, emphasizing the significance of ancient Egyptian religion for later religious developments. In it Martineau intended to "illustrate the genealogy . . . of the old faiths – the Egyptian, the Hebrew, the Christian and the Mohammedan (ibid., 279).[1] Half a century before Emile Durkheim's studies on religion and society, Martineau argued that understanding a country's religion is essential to an understanding of the country itself, and that the historical interconnections among the religions of a region such as the Middle East must be comprehended as well.

Martineau's sense of adventure and perseverance in rather uncomfortable conditions are apparent in the book. She quickly learned what to take – a pair of flat irons, a Mackintosh cloth for keeping bedding dry and to use as a carpet, washable clothes, hats (to be purchased in Cairo), fans, goggles – and recommended what not to take – European servants, a desire for sheer recreation in travel, ethnocentrism, and an inflexible attitude. She especially recommended the Levinge's bag (a muslim sleeping bag with canopy which enveloped the entire body) to promote comfort and to keep out the vermin. She coped well with living in crowded and rather primitive conditions on a dahabeah (large passenger boat) on the Nile for many weeks. She and Mrs. Yates did their laundry carefully and systematically on the boat, Harriet insisting that properly ironed linen garments were worth the effort in comfort. The boat was clean, colorful, and reasonably roomy, and staffed with several persons. While on the Nile the party enjoyed a Christmas dinner complete with turkey and plum pudding prepared by the cook. Martineau was fascinated with the interactions and singing among the crew, Nubians and Cairenes. She learned to smoke, a habit continued in later years, enjoying chibouque, a Turkish tobacco, and to ride camels in the desert which she found disagreeable in spite of her fondness for riding. A saddle, rather than wooden box or chair, improved her comfort considerably. Face-ache, caused by the desert heat and dryness, was a major problem for her. She was impressed with the multitude, if not variety, of birds in Egypt – water-wagtails, herons, pelicans, eagles, geese, the Aboo-gerdan (paddy-bird), vultures, cormorants. She was so inspired by the great temples that on more than one occasion she took brush and water and with the aid of a servant boy began scrubbing the walls to reveal the supreme art which lay below the sand. She even wished for "a great winnowing fan" to blow away the sand and uncover the great monuments of Egypt.[2] But she reflected that

It is best as it is; for the time has not come for the full discovery of the treasures of Egypt . . . the sand is a fine means of preservation . . . The minds of scholars are preparing for an intelligent interpretation of what a future age may find . . . science, chemical and mechanical, will probably supply such means hereafter, as we have not now, for treating and removing the sand (*EL*, 38).

Martineau delighted in climbing the Great Pyramid in Giza and prided herself on the fact that it took her only 22 minutes, five minutes longer than Mr. Ewart, to climb it. Of course she had the help of two Arabs. Having left her ear trumpet below, she climbed the pyramid, descended, explored the tombs and for over three hours did without the trumpet, never really missing it; "stronger proof could not be offered of the engrossing interest of a visit to the pyramid" (*EL*, 245). Always an avid walker, she frequently arose before sunrise to walk alone. Rather than ride the camel, she often walked in the desert, maintaining considerable distance between herself and the caravan to reflect on the scene and to obtain some privacy. Even the party's encounters with Bedouin bandits seemed not to deter or discourage her sense of independence and enjoyment.

Throughout the journey Martineau was fascinated with the people and their cultures, ranging from the marvel of their sculptures to the "quickness of movement, strength of frame and power of experience" of the native boys and men in the waters of the Cataract. They offered sharp contrast to "the bookworm and professional man at home, who can scarcely use their own limbs and senses, or conceive of any control over external realities" (*EL*, 73–74).

Even while studying the countries on her Eastern itinerary in pursuit of an understanding of their histories, their geographies and cultures, and their religions, Martineau shared the nineteenth-century fascination with the exotic, and, like many tourists of the period, took home her souvenir samples of the hair and the linen shroud of a mummy.

In Egypt Martineau was greatly impressed with the struggle between the Nile and the desert as geographical forces acting upon the hopes and fears of the inhabitants. The power of Osiris, manifest in the yearly rising of the Nile, to scatter his blessing was challenged by the ever-encroaching movement of sand and arid expanse, the desert. The inimitable sand persisted in its task of preserving the cultural remains of previous ages. In Sinai the rich green plains near Djebel surpassed the verdure of any site she had seen in Britain or America, and the rocky landscape at Petra appeared both desolate and romantic beyond compare. Lying within its surrounding fifteen hills and situated high enough for cool temperatures and an abundance of water, the city of Nazareth was to Martineau the most beautiful place in Palestine. In Syria she enjoyed the Cedars of Lebanon, called "Saints" by the Christians and "god-trees" by Mohammedans, spread over the green slopes of the valley leading to Eden, a village of many churches, handsome people, and abundant fruit and nut trees. She revelled in the many vistas and historical locales.

Her descriptions and analysis of life in these countries and her accounting for conditions in discussions of historical and geographical factors were impressive in their detail and sensitivity. In describing her experience of the Temple of Ramases at Abu Simbel, she writes:

98

The faces of Ramases outside are placid and cheerful – full of moral grace: but the right Osirides within are more. They are full of soul . . . The difficulty to us now is, not to account for their having been once worshipped, but to help worshipping them still. I cannot doubt their being the most abstract Gods that men of old ever adored. Instead of their being engaged in wars or mutual rivalries, or favouritisms, or toils, or sufferings, here they sit, each complete and undisturbed in his function – every one supreme – free from all passion, but capable of all mild and serene affections. The Greek and Roman appear like wayward children beside them. Herodotus says that the Greek Gods *were* children to these, in respect of age . . . and truly they appear so in respect of wisdom and maturity (*EL,* 121–22).

The culture of Egypt, "by far the most interesting portion of our travels," and the focus of nearly half of *Eastern Life,* expresses the tension between the river and the desert, between the Good One and the Evil One. The inhabitants' preoccupation with death and immortality seems to result from the interplay of the population and these natural exigencies.

The unseen world became all in all to them; and the visible world and present life of little more importance than as the necessary introduction to the higher and the greater. The imagery before their eyes perpetually sustained these modes of thought. Everywhere they had in presence the symbols of the worlds of death and life; – the limited scene of production, activity and change; – the valley with its verdure, its floods, and its busy multitudes, who were all incessantly passing away, to be succeeded by their like; while, as a boundary to this scene of life, lay the region of death, to their view unlimited, and everlastingly silent to the human ear (*EL,* 41).

Martineau links the geography to economic activities and to ideas in art and architecture, notably the "angularity of almost all forms," as in the pyramid and the obelisk. She analyzes ancient Egyptian social organization, a caste system of five to seven castes depending on the historian (*EL,* 109). In general, Martineau is deeply moved by Egyptian culture and history, and sets forth, as we shall see, her Egyptocentric theory of the history of religions. But as she travels, observes, and compares the facts of Eastern life with America, England, and Ireland, she

99

has strong criticism for such figures as Selim Pasha, a corrupt and indulgent ruler whose luxurious lifestyle came at the expense of many others, and institutions such as the hareem, the inmates of which she regarded as the most pitifully oppressed women she knew. Living lives of indolence and ignorance, she found the women of the hareem to be petty, uninteresting, and sad, deprived of any likelihood of self-realization or even basic literacy.

Martineau devotes a whole chapter to her visit to the Pasha's hareem and in later years referred often to this unforgettable instance of human oppression.

> Virtual slavery is indispensably required by the practice of polygamy; virtual proprietorship of the women involved, without the obligations imposed by actual proprietorship; and cruel oppression of the men who should have been the husbands of these women (*EL*, 299).

She criticizes Montesquieu's conclusion that polygamy is related to the early marriageability of girls who, being young, cannot satisfy the intellectual and emotional needs of their husbands. Martineau asserts that the search by a husband for another woman, "a bride and a companion of whom he may make a friend," is the effect rather than the cause of polygamy. In comparing Egypt with Turkey, "where the same religion and natural laws prevail" but where "polygamy is rare and women are not married so young," she concludes that the end of polygamy and early marriage, and improvement in the training of women, would produce greater happiness for men and freedom for women (*EL*, 299).

The sad state of women in the hareem prompted Martineau, as always, to seek some solution.

> I asked Dr. Thompson [the local physician] . . . whether he could not introduce skipping-ropes upon these spacious marble floors. I see no other chance of the women being induced to take exercise. They suffer cruelly from indigestion, – gorging themselves with sweet things, smoking intemperately, and passing through life with more than half the brain almost unawakened, and with scarcely any exercise of the limbs (*EL*, 303).

Martineau was very touched when, upon her departure,

> the chief lady gave me roses as a farewell token ... I am
> thankful to have seen a hareem under favourable circum-
> stances; and I earnestly hope I may never see another. I kept
> those roses, however. I shall need no reminding of the most
> injured human beings I have ever seen, – the most studiously
> depressed and corrupted women whose condition I have wit-
> nessed: but I could not throw away the flowers which so
> found their way into my hand as to bespeak for the wrongs of
> the giver the mournful remembrance of my heart (*EL*, 304).

In her accounts Martineau laments the lack of available statistical facts resulting from inadequacies of record keeping and
census methods in these countries. Sorely inadequate as well
are the political and social policies of the Pasha of Egypt which
resulted in illiteracy, low production and little development,
denial of civil and property rights, and a declining population.
Those civil projects, such as the Mahmoudieh canal, which did
exist were very costly in human lives and provided little toward
the development of workers' skills.

Although *Eastern Life* may be read in many ways, as we have
noted, one of its most interesting aspects is her theory of the
history and evolution of religions. Martineau's interest in religion, as reflected in her earliest writings in the *Monthly Repository*
and the 1830–31 prize essays on Unitarianism, were indicative
of her religious commitment and her sense of a personal God.
By 1830 she became acquainted with the ideas of Saint-Simon,
and thereby of Turgot and Condorcet. She read, in German,
Lessing, Herder and Kant, and it would have been surprising if
not Hegel. Denying neither the importance of religion nor the
existence of God, Martineau began increasingly to see religion,
in the tradition of the Moral Sciences, as a significant social
institution in the progress and cohesion of society, and to consider God as first but Unknowable Cause. *Eastern Life* expounds
a theory of religion as evolutionary rather than revolutionary, as
having moved through historical stages from magic, superstitu-
tion, and totemism to polytheism and then monotheism. She
seems convinced that, in the last case, unitarianism represents a
higher stage of religious evolution than trinitarianism, just as
she increasingly discussed the humanity of Jesus.

In proportion as this stage [monotheism] is passed through, the conceptions of deity and divine government become abstract and indefinite, till the indistinguishable line is reached which is supposed, and not seen to separate, the highest order of Christian philosopher from the philosophical atheist (*Auto.*, 2:280).

This progression in the development of the human mind, articulated by Turgot, *On the Successive Advances of the Human Mind* (1750), and Condorcet, *Sketch for a Historical Picture of the Progress of the Human Mind* (1795), ultimately begins in the theological stage, enters a metaphysical stage, and then progresses to a scientific understanding of the world. Reflecting on these philosophies so prevalent in her day, she internalized them and even interpreted her own intellectual evolution according to the Law of Three Stages.

Eastern Life represents an important landmark, particularly as a *public* expression of her religious views. Religion, for her, was by now a matter of investigation, of sociological understanding rather than personal revelation. As early as her study of America, she had analyzed and criticized the role of organized religion in society. The knowledge gained on her journey through the East seemed to provide the historical backdrop for her own religious views.

There were effects produced on my own character of mind which it would have been impertinent to offer there ... I never before had better opportunity for quiet meditation (*Auto.*, 2:277).

Now she was using historical, cultural, and sociological facts and observations to confirm the theory that Judaism, Christianity, and Islam evolved from, and in some respects were simply recent versions of, ancient Egyptian religion.

It was evident to me, in a way which it could never have been if I had not wandered amidst the old monuments and scenes of the various faiths, that a passage through these latter faiths is as natural to men, and was as necessary in those former periods of human progress, as fetishism is to the infant nations and individuals, without the notion being more true in the one case than in the other (*Auto.*, 2:279–80).

She points out that representations of the legends, myths, and practices of these later religions are found on the tombs and monuments of ancient Egypt, such as the annunciation of conception by the angels, scenes of judgment of one's life and character, and attainment of life after death. Martineau believed in "the progression of ideas through thousands of years, – a progression advanced by every new form of faith (of the four great forms)" (*Auto.*, 2:283). She was by now convinced that religion, like any other set of ideas, had to be viewed in its place and time. The major corruption of religion, of Christianity specifically, stems from interpeting the allegories of ancient (Egyptian) religion as literal, historical truth, so that legends or myths become history.

> If we refuse to have our faith judged by our state of society, we must not conclude on theirs [Egyptians and Arabians] by *their* state of society. If we estimate our moral ideas by the minds of our best thinkers, we must estimate theirs by their philosophers, and not by the commonalty. Insisting on this, I think I can show that we have no right to despise either their faith or their best men. I must try, in short, to show that Men's faculties exist complete, and pretty much alike, in all ages; and that the diversity of the objects on which they are exercised is of far less consequence than the exercise itself (ibid.).

Although Martineau's efforts in *Eastern Life* have been seen as wanting in detailed biblical scholarship and originality, reflecting her lack of full academic training (Pichanik, 177–8), her analysis reflected the theological debates of her day. In that respect, her book was regarded as a scandalously relativizing treatment of Christianity, on the one hand, and a brilliant adventure and analysis by an unusual woman, on the other. J.A. St. John writes in the *Westminster Review* of July 1848:

> Few persons have started so well prepared by previous travel; by familiarity with the Old and New Testaments, and profane history, ancient and modern, including the works of previous travellers; few have had their heart and soul so completely in their work; few have examined so carefully, conscientiously, and charitably, whatsoever has come to their notice; and few have shown equal power in vividly calling up the past. To

such a wayfarer in these regions, travelling is no idle pastime, no light and innocent amusement. Every step brings forth some deep significance; every scene has its absorbing and mournful interest (*WR*, 49:331–32).

The sociological perspective and holistic approach of the book resembled that of Montesquieu and demonstrated her sociological sensibilities. Reviewed in important periodicals, the book was both controversial and highly popular; it remained one of her most enjoyable efforts and treasured achievements.

During her life Martineau journeyed to, and wrote about, Scotland, the Middle East, and Ireland (twice). Her books on India and her tales set in Scandinavia, the West Indies, and elsewhere demonstrated her ability to translate travel information, geographical reports, and accounts of friends into detailed, accurate, and colorful descriptions of countries she had never visited. Her approach at home and abroad was at once that of the inquisitive traveller and the social and political analyst.

As a resident of the Lake District from the late 1840s, she was eager to write guides to the area which were then published by John Garnet in Windermere, complete with excellent geological maps by John Ruthven and drawings by T.L. Aspland and W. Banks. The guides, today still interesting and useful to the hiker and tourist in the Lake District, were intended to acquaint visitors with its natural offerings and to increase the pleasures of their holidays there. Health allowing, Martineau took a long walk every morning of her life before breakfast and work. She developed an intimate knowledge of the flora and fauna, especially the birds, of the region and provided her readers with extremely detailed and interesting information for their own explorations.

Household Education *or Child-Rearing Practices*

In 1849 Martineau published *Household Education*, a collection of articles which had appeared in a rather shortlived publication, *The People's Journal*, edited by John Saunders, and which were written to encourage consultation among all members of households who "must have a share in the family plan . . . a plan to do the best possible by each for the improvement of all." All must be instructed on the rules and methods of home life. The philosophy of the book, reflects the influence of Hartley and rests on the idea of human perfectability through moral discipline and proper use of intellect at each stage in the life cycle.

Household Education is a study of socialization, of how society transmits its values and culture and how children and even adults become acculturated. It contains many insights and some analysis and is directed particularly at parents and caretakers of children. Parents must aim for the exercise of all the powers of a child, "to take full advantage of the influences of Nature." Martineau exhibits her characteristic understanding and fondness for children. She sees the world as children experience it, often referring to her own difficulties in childhood.

She instructs parents on the care of the infirm child and the importance of sympathy and truthfulness. Her own negative experiences as a child with adults who seemed unsympathetic and often cruel were never forgotten.

I have known deafness grow upon a sensitive child, so gradually as never to bring the moment when her parents felt impelled to seek her confidence; and the moment therefore never arrived. She became gradually borne down in health and spirits by the pressure of her trouble, her springs of pleasure all poisoned, her temper irritated and rendered morose, her intellectual pride puffed up to an insufferable haughtiness, and her conscience brought by perpetual pain of heart into a state of trembling soreness – all this without one word ever being offered her by any person whatever of sympathy or sorrow about her misfortune (*HE*, 129).

Other topics included the adjustments of family members to a new baby, exercise and the care of the body, and the development of moral character.

What to teach the child?: "trust his natural moral sense and cultivate his moral taste." Humans have "no faculties which are, in themselves and altogether, evil." But instruction alone is an insufficient concern. Parents must be ever aware of the uncertainties and fears which are naturally part of the child's imagination and which may cripple the child seriously. Martineau herself suffered from fears and phobias which nearly consumed her, which were hidden from her family or, if known, were ridiculed. Considerably before Freud, Harriet Martineau analyzed the fears and anxieties of childhood and the impact of early relationships with other family members, especially parents, on the formation of the self-concepts and personal confidence of children. She wrote about the development of the faculties of perception, conception, reasoning, and imagination in children, showing how intellectual and moral powers develop together.

Martineau gave female education ("on no subject is more nonsense talked") specific emphasis, making it clear that women were capable of learning mathematics and science and that they were naturally motivated toward learning. Although she stated that educated women make better household managers, Martineau focused on women's changing situation and stressed the question of justice:

> What we have to think of is the necessity, – in all justice, in all honour, in all humanity, in all prudence, – that every girl's faculties should be made the most of, as carefully as boys'. While so many women are no longer sheltered, and protected, and supported, in safety from the world (as people used to say) every woman ought to be fitted to take care of herself. Every woman ought to have that justice done to her faculties that she may possess herself in all the strength and clearness of an exercised and enlightened mind, and may have at command, for her subsistence, as much intellectual power and as many resources as education can furnish her with (*HE*, 244).

This book was a critique rather than simply a mirror of popular mid-nineteenth-century values, a reflection of the educated middle stratum, who increasingly associated education with progress. An appreciation of the imaginative, the creative, and the emotional development of children complemented her emphasis on discipline, self-control, and good habits.

The basic truths were: "What you wish your child to be, be that to your child"; "the main point is to preserve the full confidence of the young people"(*HE*, 321); "the entire household advances together, in equal companionship, towards the great object of human existence, the perfecting of each individual in it" (*HE*, 324).

The History of England

While writing *Household Education* and a book on the Lake District, Harriet was approached by Charles Knight with the proposal that she write a history of England from 1815 to mid-century, or more specifically, that she complete a history which he had begun in serial form but found he could not continue because of the demands of business. Harriet began work on *The History of England During the Thirty Years' Peace: 1818–1846* in August 1848 and sent off the first volume in February 1849. The second volume was completed by November of the same year. This was a formidable task, and while she had some doubts about maintaining the standard set by Knight, she "joyfully agreed to work out his scheme."

The history sold well in two-volume format, having been first serialized in thirty monthly numbers (Webb 1960, 277–78). Prompted by Knight and by the book's popularity, she later wrote an introductory volume covering the years 1800–1815, and in 1863 an updated concluding section for an American edition.[3]

Harriet's thinking and writing had always reflected a strong sense of history; even in her early *Monthly Repository* essays she had analyzed the use of retrospective faculties. Her lectures to the working classes in Ambleside, begun in 1848, included several on the histories of England and America.[4] Her view of history was framed by the social and economic issues which worked themselves out in the political and domestic arenas. The threads which held it together were sociological – social continuities, progress, the influence of social institutions on one another. She understood the complexities of historical developments through the lives of individuals, their roles and ideas which were, for her, the crystallization of history. But she was constantly observing social movements and social classes and their impacts on history. Only an historically astute mind could have produced a history which was both popular among the general readership and useful to scholars such as Elie Halevy (Webb 1960, 279–80).

Martineau's history was indeed social history. She saw certain themes or peak events, we might call them, as indicators of change and of progress: Catholic Emancipation and accompanying issues of religious tolerance, the Corn Law debate and its ultimate repeal, the Reform Bill which involved the issue of participatory politics, slavery and the abolition movement. There were other burning issues of the day: education for others beside privileged white males, laws regulating domestic life, freedom of the press, capital punishment, the position of laborers, the Irish situation, Chartism. To approach each topic she focused on individuals, each of whom had served as a voice of the issues and needs of the period. Like Saint-Simon, Martineau saw society to be evolving toward a new organic period, an age of science and progress in all realms.

How did Martineau fare as an historian? George Eliot's assessment of her history of England in *The British Quarterly Review* of May 1850 probably characterizes the general view of it. She described it as not so much a history but a series of review articles; perhaps not a great composition but

> an admirable and intensely interesting book; valuable for what it brings, more valuable for what it suggests. Traces of haste, of imperfect knowledge, and of imperfect historical art, though the critic may note them, will not interfere with the admiration so justly due for its power, clearness, impartiality, and high moral tone. Miss Martineau is a remarkable writer, and this book has called forth her best qualities. Place it on your shelves: there are few modern books better worth its place (Eliot, *The British Quarterly Review* xi, May 1850, 355–71).

George Eliot wrote as late as 1852 that Harriet Martineau is "the only English woman that possesses thoroughly the art of writing" (Gordon Haight, *The George Eliot Letters* II, 1954, 32).

Professor Eli Halevy was very impressed with Martineau's *History*, as he indicated in a letter of 12 February 1927: "Miss Martineau very happily defines the real value of her work. Of course she has prejudices . . . but the prejudices are honestly avowed and are in harmony with some of the main currents of the age" (Bosanquet, 245). His view of the intention and success of her *History* was in line with Martineau's own account in her obituary. Despite her biases the *History* provides the perspective of her generation and echoes her interest in promoting education and rights for all.

Foundations for the Moral Sciences

Two significant features of the nineteenth-century British world were the predominance of bourgeois industrial (market) society and widespread doubt about human nature, society, and the universe, an aspect of the conservative romantic reaction to the Enlightenment. "Confused and unsettled" views of the world, described by J.S. Mill, alternated with attitudes of discovery, order, and certainty. The intellectual culture of the day was one of hope and dismay, optimism and anxiety.[5] The thought of Harriet Martineau reflected the ambiguities of the nineteenth-century mind. But her belief in the Law of Three Stages led her to accept "the indispensableness of science as the only source of, not only enlightenment, but wisdom, goodness and happiness" (*Auto.*, 2:330). She concluded that a philosophy based on science, a science of the laws of human nature, was needed to promote those virtues.

In the spring of 1851, following the publication of the *History* and the *Letters* with Atkinson, Martineau began her intensive study of Auguste Comte's *Cours de Philosophie Positive* (1830–42).[6] She had resolved to read rather than write for a while and was most anxious to delve into Comte who, she had heard, might have the kind of perspective or philosophy required for the age. Martineau found that Comte's original style, however "rich and diffuse," was "overloaded with words." She became convinced that his work should be condensed and translated into English for greater accessibility. The strongest inducement to embark on such an enterprise was her "deep conviction of our need for this book in my own country." She recognized the rather significant interest in science "among the working classes of this country [as] one of the most striking of the signs of the times." So, on 1 June 1852 she started work on what became a translation and condensation of the original six volumes into two. While in London with a cousin to visit the Great Exhibition, Harriet was notified by John Chapman, her publisher for the Comte project, that a Mr. Lombe, formerly of Norfolk but then living in Florence, had sent five hundred pounds for her to do that work which he himself had been prevented from doing by ill health. Harriet used the fund for expenses related to the book and invested the rest. The profits from the book sales in 1853 were divided, on her insistence, among Comte, Chapman and Martineau.

Martineau continued her rather intense social life, associating with literary figures such as Thackeray, Dickens, and Charlotte Brontë. During the two-year period of work on Comte's *Positive Philosophy*, Martineau was also involved in other projects, particularly in the numerous articles for Dickens's *Household Words*, her lectures at the Mechanics Institute in Ambleside, and articles for the *Westminster Review*. At about this time she started another novel, as relief from several imposing years of writing nonfiction. Martineau submitted the novel *Oliver Weld* through Charlotte Brontë, to George Smith, who refused to publish it because it was favorably disposed towards Catholics. "She was one of the few writers who raised a disinterested voice for religious tolerance and freedom of opinion" (Tillotson and Tillotson 1965, 324). Martineau burned the draft and related notes and returned to her work in social science. This was one of her few failures.

Martineau enjoyed her work on Comte for the same reasons she enjoyed her other undertakings, because it exposed her to new knowledge. In the evenings she studied the subjects or disciplines treated by Comte in preparation for the work of translating and condensing in the mornings ahead. Her commitment to the idea of progress through positive knowledge was thorough and heartfelt:

> I became 'strengthened, stablished, settled' on many a great point; I learned much that I should never otherwise have known, and revived a great deal of early knowledge which I might never otherwise have recalled . . . many a passage of my version did I write with tears falling into my lap; and many a time did I feel almost stifled for want of the presence of some genial disciple of my instructor, to whom I might speak of his achievement, with some chance of being understood (*Auto.*, 2:391).

Positive philosophy was, as she saw it, the only remedy for the "uncertainties of the age" which haunted and disoriented even the most enlightened and progressive of minds. "The supreme dread of every one who cares for the good of nation or race is that men should be adrift for want of an anchorage for their convictions . . . a large proportion of our people are now so adrift" (Preface to Comte, 5). If, as Martineau believed, society had entered a "critical" period from which regeneration and a new order would emerge, she believed that science itself would facilitate the "growth of knowledge and the evolution of philosophy." The social sciences, yet to be developed, would be the new basis of "intellectual and moral convictions" for not simply middle-class academics and intellectuals but the general public – the working classes as well as the bourgeoisie. The whole point of the task was an attempt on her part to make the public aware of the "great, general, invariable laws" which operate in society and which can be known only through Positive Philosophy, to inform them about the law of progress and to facilitate its realization.[7]

Martineau refused to analyze or criticize Comte's ideas in the work, stating that it would be inappropriate for her to do so. In fact, she found herself in considerable disagreement with his patriarchal, even misogynist, attitude toward women, his idea of a hierarchical society with centralized planning and control, and his advocacy of a secular religion with sociologists as high priests and Comte himself as the Pope. While his presentation of a new science of society seemed exactly what was needed, Martineau undoubtedly regarded the accompanying ideology as regressive, if not reactionary.[8]

Comte himself was so pleased with Harriet's translation that he informed her that he would replace the original with her version in his "Bibliotheque positiviste du proletaire au dixneuvieme siecle"; he was convinced that Martineau's version should be translated into French.[9] Later Comte was less enthusiastic about Martineau's work when, in his religious phase, he became aware of Martineau's agnosticism.

In 1852, while she was working on the translation and edition of Auguste Comte, Martineau travelled to Irish soil a second time. Her first exposure to Ireland had occurred during the summer of 1831 when she visited her brother James and his wife. Ireland was the subject and the title of tale no. ix of the political economy series. She had been asked by Frederick

Knight Hunt to write some leaders for the *Daily News* and subsequently agreed to send him three letters a week about her Irish travels. These letters were soon published in a volume by John Chapman under the title *Letters From Ireland*. Another volume on *The Endowed Schools of Ireland* was published in 1859. In her *History of England*, published in 1850–51, Martineau addressed the events and issues of nineteenth-century Ireland in several instances.

In the years following her work on Comte, Martineau's interest in the emerging "moral sciences" continued to grow. Writing in 1858 on the second annual congress of the National Association for the Promotion of Social Science, Martineau raised the question, "What is 'Social Science'?" In terms of her criteria, the Association had a long way to go before claiming to be involved in a scientific sociology:

> In an attempt to develop any science, whether deductive or inductive, the very first step, we conceive, is to define your subject methodically, to lay down the definition of your terms and instruments, and to ascertain what are the principles upon which the science essentially turns (*The Spectator*, October 23, 1858, 1119).

She fully realized that building a science of society would be a long and arduous process, but wished to spur on those so inclined to build in that direction. Martineau was conducting her own investigations in America, the Middle East, Ireland, on work and industry, education and the family with a high level of sociological consciousness. And her enthusiasm for the Society for the Diffusion of Useful Knowledge and later for the National Association for Social Science was predicated on the usefulness, rather than the privilege, of social science, specifically sociology.[10]

Occupation, Health and Industry

It was almost inevitable that Harriet Martineau would enter a literary relationship with Charles Dickens. The great commentator on "life in the times" had high praise for Martineau's *Society in America*, considering it to be the best book written on

America. It is not surprising, therefore, that Martineau was asked by Dickens's subeditor, W.H. Wills, to become a contributor to the new Dickens enterprise, *Household Words*. This weekly magazine for the working classes, begun in 1850, was intended to be "the gentle mouthpiece of reform." Although she had been rather critical of Dickens's fiction, particularly "his vigorous erroneousness about matters of science" with regard to the Poor Laws in *Oliver Twist*, she regarded Dickens as "capable of progress." She delighted in his *Pickwick* and thought of him as a "virtuous and happy family man" who was destined to contribute greatly to literature (*Auto.*, 2:377–79).

After a few pieces of fiction for *Household Words*, Martineau, in 1851–52, wrote a series of articles on manufacturing, subsequently reprinted in part III of her *Health, Husbandry, and Handicraft* in 1861. Although seemingly disparate in their subject matter, these articles reflect Harriet's interest in the impact of changes in technology, the division of labor, population trends, capitalism, and the money economy on the welfare and productivity of ordinary people. Other articles dealt with education, the Irish famine, and physical handicaps, and were published in *Once A Week* and *Chambers Journal* about the same time. As a social reseacher and public educator she assembled facts and statistics to inform her readers of these changes, the consequent problems, the lag between the conditions of the British population and the technical and economic revolutions occurring. The subject matter of the fifty chapters included infant survival, occupational illness, effective farming practices, and vignettes on production in a variety of industrial settings.

In several chapters she decried the treatment of children – poor nursing practices, improper diet, use of drugs on infants, and neglect which resulted in 100,000 needless deaths each year in England, 40,000 of them children under five years. She linked women's emancipation to freedom of dress, children's development to diet and exercise, and a productive, happy working class to good housing and health in the workplace. Predating the studies of Emile Durkheim, Martineau analyzed suicide, its rates and prevalence, to demonstrate the need for attention to mental and emotional health. In an attempt to dispel old ideas about suicide, i.e., that it is caused by insanity, she identified the social facts that suicide was more frequent in men, was linked to intemperance, varied according to occupation, district, and education, and was related to weak imagination and strong egotism.[11] Her recommendations were that mental illness should not be concealed but treated, and that, as heredity seemed to be a factor, cousin marriages be discouraged.

Martineau was excited about her work for *Household Words*. In 1851 she spent a month in Birmingham near her brother Robert and family, but with separate quarters to facilitate her work. She visited factories and businesses and gathered information and observed industrial production. Convinced by now that her forte lay in scientific and journalistic writing, she worked on a series on factory production – "a picturesque account of manufactures and other productive processes . . . both for instruction and entertainment" – for Dickens's *Household Words*. She wrote about electroplating, papier-maché, and the manufacture of nails and screws in Birmingham, as well as weaving and bobbin factories in Ambleside. Later she returned to Birmingham to investigate and write about several other industrial enterprises: flour mills, gold and jewelry creation, ribbon-making, needles, watches, guns, glass, brass, button, carpet, and shawl production. Other articles dealt with peat works, fishing, cheese and butter production, paper hangings, and the lead works. Martineau was excited about the prospects for new forms of industrial production. She was committed to industrial technology and even romanticized it as a boon to society.

Dickens was enthusiastic about her articles, but proceeded to edit them as he saw fit. Martineau and Dickens disagreed particularly about the industrialization and its effects on workers, about women, and about Catholicism. Eventually, Martineau came to regard Dickens as a chauvinist and as ignorant in matters of science and progress.[12] Their disagreements flared in the context of the factory controversy.

Factory Legislation

In 1854 Dickens serialized *Hard Times*, his novel about the industrial scene in England in the 1840s, in *Household Words*. In response to the novel and to some articles on factory accidents which appeared in *Household Words* in 1855, Martineau wrote *The Factory Controversy: A Warning Against Meddling Legislation*. It was originally submitted to John Chapman (the *Westmin-*

ster Review) who rejected the "attack," but was published in 1855 as a pamphlet by the National Association of Factory Occupiers, the Victorian equivalent of the American National Association of Manufacturers.

Martineau was convinced that the manufacturers were justified in resisting enforcement of the Factory Act of 1844 which required that "all parts of the mill-gearing in a factory should be securely fenced." They had interpreted the law to mean a requirement of fencing to the height of seven feet and no more, pleading that it was too costly and unnecessary to do more. They had formed an association to aid one another in the payment of fines. Dickens and others accused the factory owners of callousness in the safety of their workers, although even those who sided with Dickens recognized that it was not always possible to convince workers to take safety precautions. Dickens's reference to the mill occupiers as "The National Association for the Protection of the Right to Mangle Operatives," as well as his statistics, were challenged by Martineau as she dissected *Hard Times* in the pamphlet. She defended the employers and accused Dickens of being unscrupulous in exaggerating the threat to the workers' welfare and of poor judgment in attempting to write on political philosophy and morality (*FC,* 36). Workers, she claimed, understood the value of casings and hooks and knew that they must take precautions themselves to avoid injury. Martineau had earlier portrayed an industrial accident in one of her first political economy tales, *The Hill and The Valley,* in which a boy who had been in charge of a machine "put himself in the way of receiving a blow on the head, which killed him on the spot" (HM, *The Hill and The Valley,* 92). She argued that laws cannot protect all from everything and maintained that heavy legislation would shut down industries and thereby deprive workers and employers alike of jobs and income.[13]

The relationship between Martineau and Dickens deteriorated as she came to understand his attitudes toward and treatment of women, particularly his wife, from whom he separated in 1858. Martineau's observations on the exploitation of women in marriage and the persistent chauvinism of middle-class men seemed to her confirmed by the Dickens case.[14] They also clashed over the issue of religious tolerance when one of her stories was rejected by Dickens because it was too favorable to "Romanism." She finally terminated her association with *Household Words* in 1857 when it announced publication of a story which seemed to her obviously anti-Catholic.

Female Employment-Domestic Service

Linked to her work in political economy, Martineau had a special fascination for the variety of new occupations and industries in the economy of the nineteenth century. While completing *Deerbrook* in 1838, she prepared several mini-volumes under the general title of *The Guide to Service* as part of the "Industrial Series" published by Charles Knight for the Poor Laws Commission. This series was designed to prepare young people for occupations in trade and service. Titles included *The Maid of All Work, The Housemaid,* and *The Lady's Maid.* Martineau included in these didactic primers for domestic workers her own sociological analysis of these occupations and the social relations of employer and employee, referring, for example, to the types of female servants to be found in households of different socioeconomic standings:

> The number of maid-servants in this country is nearly a million. The largest class of all is supposed to be Maids of All Work . . . for the housekeepers who can keep only one servant. The next greatest number is of cooks and housemaids . . . The nursery maids come next [families with three female servants] . . . and ladies' maids. . . . a small class [for families who afford four female servants] (HM, *Guide to Service,* "The Ladies' Maid," 1838, 5–6).

Recognizing the changed nature of domestic employer/ employee relations within the context of new social classes, Martineau suggested that written instructions and inventories, as a sort of work contract, would clarify the performance of housework and protect both sides from arguments over duties (HM, *Guide to Service,* "The Housemaid," 1839, 28–29).

This genre of occupational and moral instruction for the working classes was an easy and favorite one for Martineau. It reflected her middle-class Protestant view that all should take work seriously at whatever "station" in society. It also afforded her opportunity to write about the changing division of labor and the specialized roles which must be carried out properly for the smooth functioning of Victorian society. Martineau maintained throughout her life that education and instruction were crucial in preparing people for life and work in this new society. She was preoccupied with themes of duty to others and to society, and work as the basis of wisdom and goodness. Furthermore, optimal existence required a balance of work and thought

> Now, if this be true, the extremely rich and the extremely poor are not the most likely to grow wise and good. The rich have too little work to do; and the extremely poor have too much work and too little thought (ibid., 81).

And so she recommended that the lady's maid memorize poetry while sewing! If her mandates seem overbearing today, it can be understood that such literature was intended to serve an educative purpose at the time. Women were increasingly employed in a variety of occupations outside the home. Country girls were taking domestic employment in towns and cities; women of all ages worked to support themselves and their families at new kinds of jobs. In her own didactic manner, Martineau wanted to instruct young British workers for successful employment. As Webb has shown in *The British Working Class Reader*, the increasingly powerful middle classes wrote such literature to inform, but also to control, the working classes in industrial society (Webb 1955).

As early as June 1838 Martineau completed a lengthy historical and social analysis of the institution of service in an article entitled "Domestic Service in England" for the *London and Westminster Review*. This article and "Female Industry" of 1859 are among her most important studies of women's work in this period.

The subject was justified by sheer numbers. Martineau demonstrated with Census data that in England female servants outnumbered male servants by seventy-five to eighteen per thousand population. After commenting on the paucity of facts on female employment, she attempted to show the underlying social causes at work, cautioning about cultural variations. It was a case of class exploitation. She described the situation of ladies of high rank gathered for a holiday in a country house, where for several days they indulge in the leisured life of the privileged while young girls serve and sew incessantly through three days and two nights, only to go unpaid in cases where their mistresses had lost their money gambling at whist (ibid., 410).

Martineau pointed out that the greatest numbers of domestic servants worked in "families of the lower rank." She described domestic service as "subjection to the will of another" for wages given as much for obedience as for industry. "Next to governesses, the largest class of female patients in lunatic asylums is Maids of All Work" (ibid., 412). The heavy work, scanty sleep, low wages, health risks and forced ingratiation cannot be understood by those who do not live by manual labor. To demonstrate her position, she compared England and America, which lacked a feudal tradition except in the South and where domestic service is by contract.

The remedies for such problems, she believed, required a redefinition of service as *honorable* and not degrading. All classes must understand the "glory of service" mutually; service must be rewarded accordingly. Reflecting her own Unitarian upbringing, she maintained that there was no place for an idle and ostentatious employer class.

Martineau's interest in the issues of domestic service continued, and in 1862 she published another analysis on "Modern Domestic Service" in the *Edinburgh Review*, in which she gave account of the types of domestic servants and their circumstances. Her solutions for the problems of isolation, alienation, and loneliness of domestics included: education in household management for employers, a court of appeal for servants with bad mistresses and masters, and training for employees in some kind of industrial schools. Domestic service remained, she thought, a form of employment only for rescuing children from pauperism and the ragged schools.

Female Employment-Industry

One of Martineau's most detailed expositions on women and work appeared in *The Edinburgh Review* in April 1859 (151–73). Entitled "Female Industry," it was a review of several British and American works on women ranging from the British Census of 1851 to *The Lowell Offering*. Martineau brought together statistical, historical, and sociological facts to address the changes in women's industrial work. It was a comprehensive and thoughtful analysis of the labor of women and the issues which needed to be addressed to correct inequities. She laid to rest the myths that women are supported economically by men and that women's activities do not constitute labor or paid work. She emphasized that fifty percent of women (three million out of six million in Great Britain at that time) were breadwinners, nearly two-thirds of those (or two million) self-supporting. She showed that women were affected by the changes in technology and in the division of labor as much as men, and should be given serious consideration as breadwinners. Her brief history of women's work took into account the long and heavy labor of household and family industry by women in every social class, including many kinds of female employment in healing and health care, agriculture, fishing and shipping, mining, industry, and numerous new occupations.

Urbanization involved a movement of women to the cities for work, a situation which increased remarkably the ratio of women to men there. The independence of female labor in domestic work was established by the fact that women who became domestic wage earners in middle-class homes not only had less access to marriageable men (she shows with 1851 census figures), but may also have preferred remaining single to the "precarious independence of married life." The sad truth was that a large proportion of domestic workers belonged to poor families, and they had little to provide for themselves in old age.

Martineau reported that occupations in the service and commercial industries were increasingly populated by women who worked as nurses, matrons of asylums, hospitals, and gaols, lighthouse keepers, pew-openers, waiters, shopkeepers, and shopwomen. In some occupations, as in shops, women were seen as a threat to men. In accountancy and business management, as well as in telegraphing, printing, bookbinding, textile manufacturers, and the hotel and boardinghouse trade, women were becoming more numerous. She noted that, although women in the commercial classes were usually widows who had previously assisted their husbands as shopkeepers, innkeepers, dairy merchants and the like, English women typically did not remain in business long because of their financial ignorance; whereas in

France and the United States women seemed to prosper in business "at least as well as men" (ibid., 160).[15] That women were capable in mathematics but simply lacked training was shown by the rising numbers of women accountants. Women, particularly but not only in Britain, needed better training and education to enable them to take their places in the new division of labor and to manage their affairs independently.

Martineau gave considerable attention to the employment of women in the textile manufactures, who numbered 385,000 in 1851. Women who must stay at home could benefit from paid work there such as watchmaking (in Switzerland). But she recognized that male guilds of watchmakers in England would not allow it.

> It seems incredible that some thousands of foreign women should be supported by making watches for us to buy dear, while thousands of needlewomen should be starving in London, for want of permission to supply us with cheaper watches (ibid., 168).

Martineau recognized that women's disadvantages in the labor force resulted from men's desire to dominate in matters of paid work. Exclusion from watchmaking, design, and medicine, as well as harshness and harassment in the factory were the consequences of jealousy and discrimination by males. The only widely available occupation for women was that of governess. Although governesses were usually single, most were supporting family members, paying for their brothers' schooling or their fathers' debts. In fact, "the proportion of governesses who have the advantage and use of their own earnings is very small" (ibid., 170).

Martineau's suggestions for improving women's position in the work force included education and nondiscriminatory employment and training practices in industry. She emphasized that occupations in medicine should be opened to women and supported by proper training. "The health of women and children will never be guarded as it ought to be till it is put under the charge of physicians of their own sex." She advocated that medical colleges for women be established, as in the United States, and emphasized the importance of physical fitness and exercise for girls and women. Indeed, one of the books reviewed in this essay was *The Laws of Life, with Special Reference to the Physical Education of Girls*, 1858, by Elizabeth Blackwell, the first woman physician in America.

Martineau understood and analyzed society as an "objective" observer. Like other social investigators, she was interested ultimately in a cohesive social order and the improvement of people's lives, which for her included such matters as food production and diet, the physical and social attributes of dress, care of infants and the rights of the aged, the prevention of suicide and other social problems, cooperatives and experimental communities, and the development of social science in Britain.

Colonialism

Martineau's fascination with international affairs, apparent in some of the early tales and continued in such works as *Eastern Life, Letters from Ireland, The Hour and The Man*, was sustained over the years as she took up the social and political issues of modernity.

Certainly the issue of colonialism was a recurrent one as Martineau and her contemporaries sought resolutions to the problems of the Empire and Britain's relations with its various sectors. In that regard Ireland and India occupied most of her attention. Martineau's opinions on the problems of the two countries echoed imperialism and dogmatism (Webb 1960, 334–39). She criticized Mill's proposal for peasant ownership of land and favored, instead, emigration and education as solutions to Ireland's problems. But she had persistent sympathy for the Irish, whom she believed to be abused by English policy, the Church of England, and regressive economic measures. She understood the strengths of the Irish, especially the women, whom she praised for having worked hard and having held Irish society together. She was a defender of their commitment to Catholicism as she took the side of religious tolerance. Nonetheless, she supported the capitalization of Irish agriculture and dispersal of part of the Irish population to other lands to find employment as constructive ways of pulling Ireland out of its misery. It was in the cultivation of a middle class, a bourgeoisie, that Ireland would save itself, she alleged. Similar issues were reflected in her analyses of the situation in India.[16]

In later writings, including *British Rule in India* (1857), *Suggestions Towards the Future Government of India* (1858), and numerous leaders in the *Daily News*, within the limits of her generally liberal and imperialist posture, she exhibited a strong sensitivity toward Indian society, its customs and institutions.[17] Martineau wished to convey to her readers the facts of geography, history, military excursions, and government to advance their understanding of the circumstances of the Mutiny. In *Suggestions* . . . , which followed a year later, she made a more specifically sociological analysis of the situation which dealt with the difficulties of religious and cultural differences and with the need for the British to understand more thoroughly the cultural ethos and complexities of Indian society.

> Never was there a more difficult case – never a more portentous conjunction in human history, than this arbitrary co-existence of the European and Asiatic genius on the same soil. We were only strangers in the country, living there first for self-interest, and next for duty; and never from any sympathy for, or real intercourse with the inhabitants (HM, *Suggestions*, 33).

Nevertheless, Martineau supported the British rule which, she claimed, saved India from anarchy, wars, and misrule. "The people have been led up to a point of progress at which they cannot stand still." She suggested that two things must be done: the British must learn about and care more about India, and, on the basis of knowledge about that society (its institutions, history, geography, etc.), Britain must act in a way to bring India into the modern age.[18]

Ultimately, Martineau's "solutions" to the situations in Ireland and India centered on education and entrepreneurial capitalism, which she thought the British had a responsibility to promote in both countries. It was the rationalist argument that science, knowledge, and disciplined economic behavior would save inhabitants in both cases from the crises and conflicts generated, she thought, by traditional culture. At the same time, however, Martineau understood that colonialism creates domination and double standards, and that the impact of the colonizer upon indigenous populations is a serious matter.

Behavior in the colonies was, she thought, a manifestation of the problems and inequities in British society itself. In discussing the need for improvement in political relations between Indians and the British, Martineau commended the work of the East India Company and regretted the fact that Indians seemed to know the British presence only through the military. In fact, the weakening of Indian power structures threatened traditional Indian society, prepared the favored few only for military careers, and barred those with professional ambitions from realizing them. The approach reflected British imperialism and paternalism.

> We have been too much given at home, as well as everywhere else, to a priori speculation about the 'sphere' of our inferiors, be they who they might; and the Irish Catholics, the American colonists, and English ploughmen, artisans, and women, have all had more or less of the experience which the Hindoos and Mussulmans of Hindostand are suffering under, of having their 'sphere' (a very contracted one) pronounced on by the dogmatists who appropriate a higher 'sphere' (HM, *Suggestions*, 93).

In all of Martineau's writings, her own concerns that the disadvantaged of the world, either by physical, age, gender or economic handicaps, be treated fairly and be given genuine understanding are evident. To her, the prejudices and discrimination which assign people and expectations for their behavior to remote corners of the social order, to "spheres," were systemic. Quite clearly, she understood the relations among these injustices.

Foreign policy was a vital matter for Britain, she thought, and she proffered the liberal position that secret diplomacy must be abolished and Parliament must be accountable to the people. There was a need for a balance of power and policy of principle.

> It is because we have no fixed and avowed principle and rule that our conduct is vacillating and uncertain; and it is because foreign nations never know what we shall do next, that they have so little respect for our doings, and that we have lost almost all power of peaceful remonstrance (ibid., 204).

In her analysis Martineau recognized the differences between the cultures of the East and of the West – the dominance of tradition, on the one hand, and of rationality, on the other. But she believed that peace and progress could be assured by the nations sharing and participating in the new scientific and technological culture. She saw colonialism and its heroes as manifestations of the natural laws of progress. And she expressed the conviction of her generation, that the law of progress would emancipate society from "the burdens of the past" (Houghton: 45ff. See HM, "England's Foreign Policy", *WR*, 61, January 1854, 191).

Notes

1. Note that all page references to *Eastern Life* are to the one-volume edition published by Moxon in 1850.
2. As the David Roberts lithographs of Egypt show, the great monuments were largely buried in sand in the mid-nineteenth century.
3. The book was published under the title *The History of England from the Commencement of the XIXth Century to the Crimean War* in four volumes. Her sources included Hansard, the Annual Register, periodicals and books of all sorts, particularly autobiographies and biographies. See Webb for a good discussion of Martineau's historical writing, esp. 277–82.
4. During several winters Martineau gave lectures and courses in the local Mechanics Institute in Ambleside to members of the working class as part of her attempt to educate and qualify workers for fuller participation in society.
5. See Houghton, 22–23.
6. Comte is considered the father of French sociology, if not the discipline of sociology in general, probably because he named the field and was the first to outline in detail its focus and scope. He developed his system of sociological positivism in private lectures given over several years in Paris, although he never held a regular academic appointment. The volumes were written and published between 1830 and 1842. The aims of his *Cours de Philosophie Positive* were to outline the hierarchy of the sciences, to show their development historically as well as the methods and findings in each as relevant to the whole positive system, and to show that the sciences of observation now needed a final science-social physics or sociology (Comte, 31). Recently his claim to this title has been questioned. In fact, Comte's (mis)understanding of the positivism

of his day in currently under review. He drew heavily from Turgot and Saint-Simon, among others, for his ideas.

7. Professor John Nichol of Glasgow reviewed the sections on Mathematics, Astronomy, and Physics; and Harriet made significant changes to the section on Physics only in the form of condensation.

8. In his early years Auguste Comte proclaimed that Sociology would prove that women are physically, emotionally, and intellectually inferior to men. Years later he fell in love with a married woman, Clothilde de Vaux, who was apparently equally fond of him, but who become ill and died within a year. Thereafter, Comte gave greater consideration in his theories to love and the moral perfection of women (the pedestal) and accorded them a higher place in his utopian scheme in his *Systeme de Politique Positive* (1851–54).

9. This was done by C. Avezac-Lavigne and published in France in 1871 and 1872.

10. As Robert Webb has observed, "for years she had been preaching sociology without the name" (Webb, 308).

11. In fact, she had developed a typology of suicides in her treatise of 1838 on *How To Observe Manners and Morals* which anticipates the very categories of Durkheim's analysis: suicides based upon shame ("fatalism"), complete devotion to others ("altruism"), honor ("egoism"), and withdrawal from duty and expectations of others ("anomie").

12. See HM's letter to Fanny Wedgwood, 20 October 1860, Arbuckle, 195–200. Although she was probably correct in both assessments, Dickens did greet industrial capitalism enthusiastically and professed, along with others in his generation, his belief in progress.

13. Hyppolyte Taine's review of *Hard Times* in 1856 anticipated Martineau's position, when he said of Dickens, "he exalts instinct above reason, intuition of the heart above positive knowledge; he attacks education built on statistics, figures, and facts." Quoted in "Introduction" by Philip Collins to Dickens, *Hard Times*, 1978, vii).

14. For an interesting analysis of the Dickens marriage, see Phyllis Rose, *Parallel Lives: Five Victorian Marriages*, (New York: Random House, 1984), 148–91.

15. Statistical evidence indicates that Martineau was correct in identifying the disparities between England and France (and Germany) regarding women's participation in commerce and finance, as seen in Laura Frader, "Women in the Industrial Capitalist Economy" in *Becoming Visible: Women in European History*, second edition, edited by Renate Bridenthal et al. (Boston: Houghton Mifflin, 1987), especially 316–18.

16. As early as 1832 Martineau wrote in the *Monthly Repository* about India in a review of works by Rajah Rammohun Roy, who had recently visited England and, as a convert to Christianity, seemed to be particularly popular among Unitarians. The article was a stern critique of British policy in India. It called attention to the exploitation, poor conditions, and general political oppression of

Indians resulting from imperialism. The disruption of traditional institutions like the Puchayet (a local jury which provided justice and arbitration in disputes and general access to courts), the exploitative land and tenure and revenue systems, and the generally saddened state of the population required enlightened policies rather than domination. But "the best hope for India" was the hastening of English settlers to improve both land and labor, to show the native inhabitants the "superior methods of cultivation and the proper mode of treating their laborers and dependents" (*MR* September 1832, vi: 614).

17. *British Rule in India* was originally written as among the many leaders for the *Daily News* she wrote between 1852–66.
18. Martineau's views on India are summarized in Webb, 340–45.

Plate 1. Harriet, c. 1830. Courtesy of The Bodleian Library.

Plate 2. Octagon (Unitarian) Chapel, Norwich.

Plate 3. Harriet Martineau, 1834. Original oil painting by Sir R. Evans. Courtesy of the National Gallery.

Plate 4. Plaque commemorating Harriet's birthplace in Norwich in Gurney Court house, which was also the birthplace of Elizabeth Fry.

Plate 5. Courtyard view of Martineau home, Gurney Court, Norwich.

Plate 6. Harriet Martineau, 1849. Drawing by
George Richmond. Courtesy of the National Gallery.

Plate 7. Ambleside, nineteenth century.

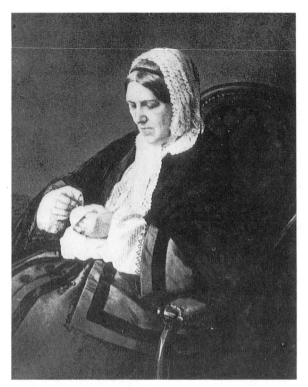

Plate 8. Martineau at Ambleside.

Plate 9. The Knoll, Ambleside.

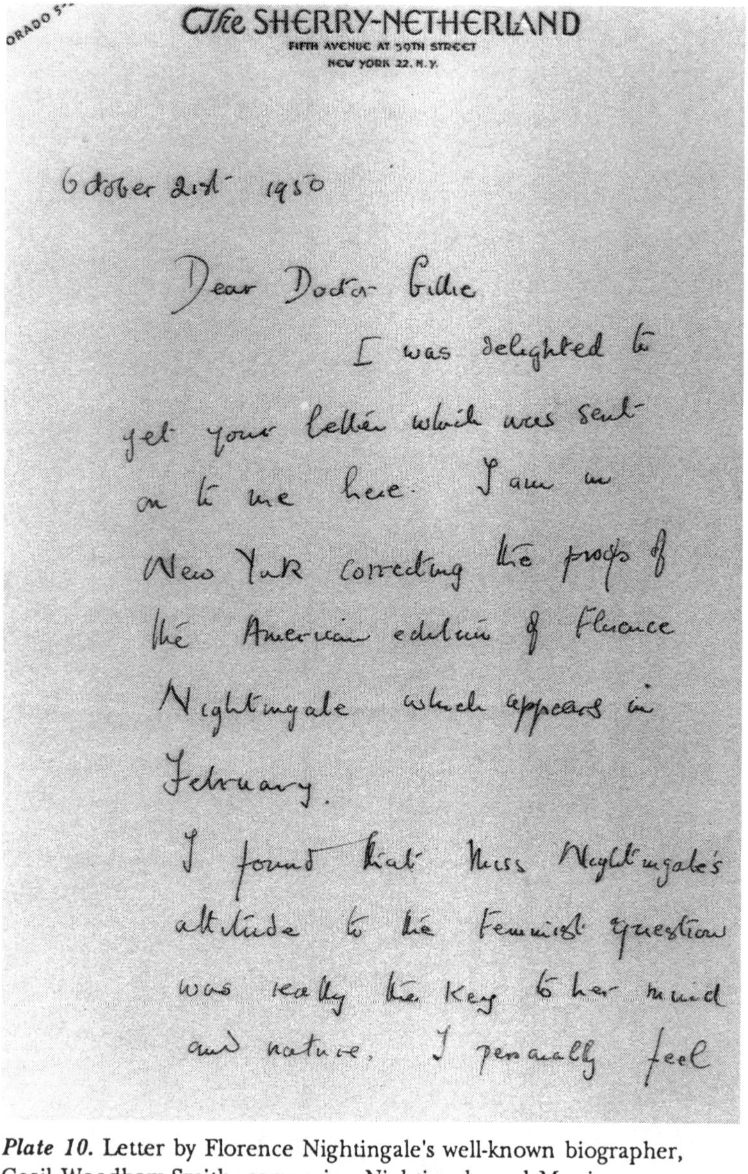

The SHERRY-NETHERLAND
FIFTH AVENUE AT 59TH STREET
NEW YORK 22, N.Y.

October 21st 1950

Dear Doctor Gillie

I was delighted to get your letter which was sent on to me here. I am in New York correcting the proofs of the American edition of Florence Nightingale which appears in February.

I found that Miss Nightingale's attitude to the Feminist question was really the key to her mind and nature, I personally feel

Plate 10. Letter by Florence Nightingale's well-known biographer, Cecil Woodham-Smith, comparing Nightingale and Martineau.

much more sympathy with her than with,
for instance, the admirable Harriet
Martineau. I know nothing about the
medical aspect but do you not think
the fact that Miss Nightingale - up to
the end of her life, had the power to
charm men, I mean quite simply that
they fell in love with her, does set her
quite apart from women, again like
Harriet Martineau, who never had the
equipment (or perhaps the glands?!!)
to do this

My husband wishes to be
remembered to you

Yours sincerely

Cecil Woodham-Smith

Plate 11. Martineau in her later years. Courtesy of the National Gallery.

AUTUMN

6 The Journalist *Par Excellence*

> The want of independence of mind, the shutting
> their eyes and professing to believe what they do
> not, the running blindly together in herds, for fear
> of some obscure danger and horror if they go alone,
> is so eminently a vice of the English, I think, of the
> last hundred years ... that I cannot but praise a
> person whose one effort seems to have been to deal
> perfectly honestly and sincerely with herself.
> —Matthew Arnold on Harriet Martineau, 1855

Harriet Martineau's prodigious writing career continued into
its fourth decade at a relentless pace. By the early 1850s she had
published perhaps two-thirds of her total volumes. After completing the *History of England* (1849, 1851), the *Letters* ... with
Atkinson (1851), and the translation of Comte's *Positive Philosophy* (1853), she felt an ever keener desire to address the present, to help in some way to influence the British ship of state in
international waters and in its own internal affairs. She had
been prompted by the emergence of certain issues which she
felt required immediate and informed attention (slavery in the
United States and the threat to the Union, the British presence
in India, the Irish famine, the status of women, and education).
Furthermore, she had become an analyst of some influence.
She was drawn into journalism in the 1850s, and out of "retirement" again in the late 1860s largely by her own view of her
life's mission as a public educator, but also by the continual
requests for her advice, support, and intervention on behalf of
social causes, political issues, and diplomatic matters.

At a time when an accomplished author might have turned
her attention to the quiet leisure of domestic life and to the
care of her always precarious health, Harriet Martineau turned
to her fourth career, journalism, not exactly deliberately but, it
seemed, inevitably.

The new career provided additional income during several
years of some economic uncertainty. Martineau had on more
than one occasion refused the offer of a government pension,

even though she clearly needed money, particularly during her years of illness. She did not approve of such government supports for those who were not desperate; more importantly, she felt that accepting the pension would somehow constrain her, diminishing her freedom as a commentator on issues involving government policy and legislation. Nevertheless, her financial status was of concern to her and others during her illness in the 1840s and again in the late 1860s.[1]

Victorian Periodicals

Although Martineau had contributed to various periodicals from the beginning of her writing career, in the 1850s and 1860s particularly she published increasingly in periodicals and became a regular contributor to the *Daily News*. Several of Martineau's later books were actually published collections from periodicals to which she contributed. It is indicative of her popularity that publishers were interested in republishing her articles in monograph form. Martineau communicated cogently and unequivocally on the significant topics of the day; she never rewrote her material. Confident and often dogmatic, she quickly worked out her analysis of a situation or event and plunged into the public debate.

Among the periodicals which published her work were *The Athenaeum, Cornhill Magazine, Edinburgh Review, Macmillan's Magazine, Quarterly Review, Once A Week, Pall Mall Gazette, Penny Magazine, People's Journal*, the *Westminster Review*, and its predecessor the *London and Westminster Review, The Leader, The Spectator*. In addition, she wrote 90 letters in The *National Anti-Slavery Standard* and papers on army hygiene for *Atlantic Monthly*. Perhaps her most important association was with the liberal *Edinburgh Review*, edited by her cousin Henry Reeve (1813–95), where she became a regular contributor. Reeve became her close friend and correspondent for many years.

The subject matter of her articles was broad and reflected a growing focus on sociological issues. Although her contributions are too voluminous and diverse to describe in detail here, a sample of her work will suffice. For example, in complementary articles in *Cornhill Magazine* in 1864 she examined and criticized the education of middle-class boys and girls. Supporting the Social Science Association's call for a government commission to inquire into the quality of education for the middle classes, she extolled the virtues of some of the Dissenter's institutions, pointed out the weaknesses of British public schools and warned that heavy reliance on the State for answers to educational problems would lead to a deterioration of England's best qualities. It was an appeal to make education relevant for the emerging society. In an eloquent plea for the education of girls she lamented the traditional approach which prepared them for domestic affairs and neglected languages and sciences. Tracing the evolution of education for middle-class girls, as she had done for boys, she showed that education for gentility was totally dysfunctional for the middle-class women of her day.

> Without the society of equals, and the impulse and discipline of extensive companionship, girls can no more have their powers developed and their qualities ascertained than boys can. Nobody believes that a boy, or a family of brothers, could become what men ought to be by an education by a tutor at home, without school or college. Girls are, under such a system, as surely as boys, doomed to be priggish, conceited, one-sided, superficial, and either languid or full of partisan tendencies (ibid., 555).

As a middle-class woman, she had always been concerned about the fate of the "daughters of educated men," but she emphasized the necessity to prepare women of all classes for an independent life. Although she considered English education to be inferior to French education, she was hopeful that quality education in England could be obtained without sacrificing English manners and tastes. Education in America particularly fascinated her, in large part because of its democratic nature. She was greatly encouraged by the emergence of female institutions in America, such as Vassar, where women had greater advantage and freedom to pursue their studies, and she strongly supported the establishment in Britain of Queen's College and Bedford College, as well as the setting of Cambridge exams for women.

Martineau wrote numerous articles on women and work, pointing out that nearly one-third of the women over twenty years of age were employed as independent workers; and among single and widowed women four-fifths were self-supporting. In several instances she wrote about the profession of nursing ("Nurses Wanted," *Cornhill*, 1865 and "Miss Nightingale's Notes on Nursing," *Quarterly Review*, April 1860). Florence Nightingale was working to establish nursing as a profession for women; and Harriet Martineau was one of her strongest supporters.

Other articles dealt with labor legislation in the Acts of 1824 and 1825, and expressed views of unionization as a violation of freedom of contract, secret trade organizations as conspiratorial toward nonmember laborers and possibly society itself, and machine production as superior to piecework. She generally took the side of the factory occupiers, but she was convinced also that strikes, resistance to technology, and use of workers' monies to resist change and "retard worker advancement" were interferences with the natural laws of progress and, as a utilitarian, with the best results for all. She wrote about the "Convict System in England and Ireland," "Life in the Criminal Class," "Cooperative Societies in 1864" and "Results of the Census of 1851."

She was interested in prison reform and the rehabilitation of youth before they became hardened criminals. The subject had first captured her attention in 1832, when she published an article on prison discipline in the *Monthly Repository*. [2] She called for an enlightened attitude toward punishment in an advanced civilization and for education of the populace as an antidote to crime. She supported the aims of the Prison Discipline Society to administer sentences and punishment appropriate to the crime, to separate prisoners according to an informed system of classification (taking age, class, character, crime into account), to speed up the trial process, and, above all, to improve and rehabilitate the prisoner. Her major concern was to prevent further corruption of criminals because she considered England to have failed in that regard.

She exercised her sociological skills well in an important article entitled "Results of the Census of 1851," which appeared in *The Westminster Review*, April 1854, and which presents a social-economic history of Great Britain from antiquity through the feudal system to the emergence of the class system and industrial society. The theme is reminiscent of Adam Smith: that population increase is an indication of the progress and prosperity of a society. Martineau saw America, however, as faster growing and more progressive than Britain. Included in her analysis was a discussion of the major demographic findings and of the methodological complications in taking the first census of Britain.

Her articles in *The Spectator* and in *Once a Week*, signed "From the Mountain," included both fiction and nonfiction. In these she wrote about relief for distressed "workies" in Lancashire, important philosophers, merchants, political agitators, men of letters, murders in Sheffield, many topics concerning women, and, of course, America and slavery.

The Daily News

In April 1852 Harriet Martineau was asked by Frederick Knight Hunt, editor of the *Daily News*, if she would be interested in sending him an occasional leader (editorial page article). She agreed, and was so delighted by the "noise" which her first submissions created that, convinced by Knight that more were desired, she agreed to do two leaders per week, and later three. The early columns included her 1852 letters from Ireland.

In these leaders we see Martineau's journalistic talents as she captures succinctly the significance of topical events and trends. In many respects this particular commitment provided a renewal of her contacts in London and with people in other places. Martineau enjoyed being immersed in observations of, and debates over, current affairs. The early death of Mr. Hunt in 1854 was a blow to her, but she continued to work well with his successors, William Weir, Thomas Walker, and John Robinson, until 1866 when she had to withdraw for reasons of poor health.

Journalism was a particularly attractive career for Martineau. As in her other endeavors, she was prolific, writing between May 1852 and April 1866 a total of 1,642 leaders. The work required daily reading and commentary on current events and issues, creating additional demands on Martineau but also enlarging her influence on the reading public.

These leaders covered an astonishing range of subjects: emigration to Australia, British foreign policy (particularly in India), slavery in America and American politics, agricultural practice and policy on cattle disease and cotton crops, education, juvenile delinquency, reformatories, working-class diets, industry and labor relations, the Crimean War, and especially the work of Florence Nightingale, European politics, the problems of Ireland, women and work, education and marriage, the National Association for the Promotion of Social Science, and so on.[3] They concerned the major conflicts of the time, including the Crimean War, the Mutiny in India, and the American Civil War.

In several *Daily News* leaders in April 1857 she made the case for a national education policy for the education of both sexes. National education was required to establish among the population "virtue based on principle." Like Marx, Martineau stressed the connection between education and productive labor; and she commended those colleges in America where both mental and manual labor were considered necessary for a proper education. Martineau recognized the significance of work for self-definition and self-development. In 1857, in writing about the American economic crash and the importance of women's work in coping with it, she emphasized how their efforts "help to show the nobleness of labor and the vulgar instability of idle luxury."

At the same time Martineau expressed positions which alienated potential supporters and created among some the image of Martineau as classist and uncaring. For example, she made it clear that she did not approve of the fencing of machinery beyond minimal requirements on the grounds that the costs to occupiers (owners) would lead to laying off of some employees and perhaps ultimate closure of many factories. She was ambivalent about trade unions and against strikes but favorable toward cooperative societies, because they demonstrated to her that cooperation can be more effective and less expensive than competition in providing women and men with work and the means to meet their cultural, personal, and economic needs. She suggested that the availability of credit and the participation in capital growth by workers would decrease scarcity. She maintained that credit for the working classes in Rochdale and in Lancashire and Yorkshire would aid in consumption, including the use of cultural institutions like libraries, schools, and public baths, and would help to generate capital from investments. She approved of cooperative dining halls and food services for the home, anticipating "The Grand Domestic Revolution" of the 1870s and 1880s.[4]

Martineau's *Daily News* leaders indicate that her objections about safety measures in factories, a shorter work week, and government control over conditions in collieries and health measures softened somewhat over the years. Her intransigence on these issues has been exaggerated. Although committed to the idea that a worker's right to labor is inalienable, she agreed, as in the case of Graham's proposed Factory Bill of 1843, that education must be provided by government for those who are incapable of demanding it, or even of realizing in advance its importance (*History*, 2:557–59; 90–91, 408). Likewise, as in the case of relief for Lancashire workers unemployed because of cotton famine, she felt that those who are unable to help themselves must be given assistance. Martineau was always in favor of efforts or measures on behalf of those who could not act for themselves – children, rural workers, the poor and women. Nevertheless, she condemned, begging and street charity as extorsive and unproductive (*DN* January 12 and March 24, 1856).

In the 1850s Martineau reiterated her views on the importance of social science for the progress of society. She was very interested in the emergence in 1857 of the National Association for the Promotion of Social Science. Under the leadership and support of George W. Hastings and Lord Brougham, the Association was formed by members of the British Association for the Advancement of Science who wished to study political economy, education, and social issues, and who had received less than enthusiastic support from their science colleagues to study "social laws." The membership included both women and men, who met annually to hear papers and exert pressure for legislative reform and general societal improvements.

While the Association's original purpose was to study society, during its twenty-nine years of existence (1857–86) it was primarily concerned with social reform. The annual congresses attracted 1,500 to 2,000 participants: merchants, industrialists, economists, clergy, bankers, lawyers, philanthropists, civil servants, members of Parliament, and social workers. Martineau was not a member, primarily for reasons of poor health and decreasing mobility, but she watched the growth of the association with interest and wrote about its work.[5] Her childhood friend, Mary Carpenter, was very active in the association, contributing thirty-two papers to their meetings over a twenty-year period, all of them read by men (McCrone, 47).

Although Martineau undoubtedly supported the work of the association and approved of the issues which it addressed, particularly women's issues, as early as 1858 she registered her skepticism of its scientific efficacy. According to Martineau, a clear conception of the term "science" was needed; science meant more than knowledge, and therefore the Association was claiming to promote something which did not yet exist.

> Social science does not yet exist, while knowledge on social subjects abounds more than it ever did before in any age . . . In its true philosophical sense, science means a recognition of the bases of knowledge, of the laws of facts . . . The true science of society is the establishment of the laws under which mankind lives in society; and those laws must be derived from the nature of Man. This nature is not yet ascertained: that derivation has not yet been traced (*DN* October 25, 1858, 4).

Her concerns were, in fact, borne out. The organization seemed designed to inform the privileged classes, assuage their guilt about being privileged, and promote certain reforms for the lower classes, with whom they could not really identify, within the industrial capitalist context of that time. Nevertheless, the organization educated the public and influenced legislation on numerous social issues (McCrone, 45–46). Martineau criticized the name rather than the actual activity or purpose of the Association, for she saw value in its ameliorative function. Unlike its parent, the Association for the Advancement of Science, the NAPSS was, and should be seen to be, a practical enterprise:

> It is true, the best practice must proceed from sound theory; and sound theory must be established by speculation; but no desultory association can undertake this highest work; and it may well be satisfied at present with devising meliorations of social ills, and organising improvements of social advantages (ibid.).

In 1859 Martineau gave the Association high marks for dealing with topics which she thought important – mercantile legislation, the bankruptcy law, the cruelties endured by merchant seamen in British-American commerce, and most urgently, the problems of labor, especially in the oppressive trade societies. She praised the work of the Association for its involvement of women and its concern with women's issues, including the effects of factory life on women and the subject of women's education. Ironically, although the discussions and activities of members on such issues as married women's property rights, women's entrance to the Cambridge exams, paid employment for middle-class women, mothers' custody rights, and treatment of prostitutes had contributed significantly to favorable resolutions, women were excluded from the power structure of the Association (McCrone, 47–58).

Biography and Autobiography

Martineau's prodigious journalism included obituaries and biographical portraits of friends and well-known persons in all walks of life. Many of her memorials were written years before the demise of their subjects, a fact which left uneasy feelings in some of those mortal beings. John R. Robinson, editor of the *Daily News*, suggested the publication of a collection of these memoirs, and in 1869 a volume entitled *Biographical Sketches* of literary, scientific, social, political, and royal figures was issued in England and America.[6] The sketches featured, among others, Charlotte Brontë, John Croker, John Lockhart, Mary Wordsworth, Thomas De Quincey, Lord Macauley, Anna Jameson, George Combe, Alexander von Humboldt, Sir Frances Beaufort, David Roberts, Lady Byron, Mary Berry, John Murray, James Elgin, Henry John Palmerston, Henry Brougham, Metternich, and Frederick William IV.

While mentioning their accomplishments and contributions, she did not hesitate to analyze personalities and assess character. In her commentary on her dear friend Charlotte Brontë, for instance, she criticized Brontë's "overemphasis" on love in women's lives. "Her heroines love too readily, too vehemently . . . but they do their duty through everything" (*BS* 1876, 363). In a piece on Jane Marcet, Martineau extols Marcet's writings on natural science and political economy as well as her children's stories, while commenting that "her pleasure in this kind of intercourse with childlike minds somewhat impaired the quality of her later works . . . which are . . . too much of the garrulous order" (ibid., 389–90).

In her insightful passages Martineau portrayed the distinctiveness of character which gave a sense of familiarity to the reader. She appreciated and revealed the strength of character and love of others of Lady Byron, the dedication to art of David Roberts, the extraordinary talents in science of Mrs. Somerville, whose life was rather sadly spent in Italy away from scientific colleagues and the apparatus of science she required. Although Martineau assigned the faults in Somerville's work to "want of a masculine training of the faculties," she gave due recognition to Somerville's books on astronomy, physical sciences, and geography, and, most of all, to her general intellectual efforts which continued until her death (ibid., 494).

The *Sketches* illustrate Martineau's view of history, framed as it was by the lives and contributions of individuals of outstanding character or accomplishment. Unitarianism and some exposure to Calvinism had taught her that those who take duty and individual responsibility seriously, who have, in short, a sense of vocation, make a difference in the world. They may or may not influence world events, but they do appear as representatives of the virtues, values, and goals which serve human progress.[7] She saw individuals as representatives and carriers of particular ideas, orientations to the world, causes and plans of action. They were for her the messengers of progress.

Martineau's view was that history and biography were so intertwined that we could understand the one only through knowledge of the other. The Victorian consciousness of the individual in history made autobiography probably the most popular of Victorian genres. As we have tried to show, Martineau's writing was autobiographical in many respects. It is not surprising, then, that in 1855, when Martineau had become quite ill again and believed she had little time to live, she interrupted her journalism for three and a half months to write her memoirs.

She wanted to control the record of her life. She requested of family and friends that her letters be burned or returned. She also composed and filed, ready for press, her own obituary. There were grounds for desiring this control. From the earliest years of her life Harriet Martineau felt misunderstood and controlled, first by her mother, then by her brother James, to whom she had been so devoted and on whom she had relied prior to his public rebuke by publishers, who frequently exacted unfair agreements which they then sometimes failed to honor, and sometimes by the public. It was with great effort and determination, and with some resistance from her family, that she had established a life of her own, to work and to live as she preferred. Even in illness, when she took the decision to explore mesmerism to relieve her physical suffering, she was shunned by her family and some friends.

To assure full control over her autobiography, she had it printed and bound, ready to be distributed upon her death. While this guaranteed that her views on the world and her self-understanding would be preserved, it precluded additions or changes in the document to reflect the last twenty years of her life. Martineau appointed Maria Chapman trustee of her papers and the memoir itself. Although Mrs. Chapman had maintained a long correspondence with her, this has always seemed a curious choice. Maria Chapman's "Memorials" volume which accompanies the autobiography is sentimental and in many respects inconsistent with Martineau's own temperament. Martineau may have assumed that she would get fairer and more objective treatment from her friend in America, who would not prejudge her from some particular British viewpoint. A woman who was completely convinced of the importance of objective history, empirical knowledge, and facts derived through positive method, Martineau wanted to insure that her own understanding and interpretation of her experience and actions would be preserved. The *Autobiography* is probably her most widely read work.

In her writings she uses her own personal experience as the ground for exploring new knowledge and insights into human relations. She developed her epistemological perspective from her particular position as a middle-class Victorian woman, an agnostic, and a positivist. In her view, rationalism and historical understanding were the keys to a clarification of social issues, which involved a weaving of life and knowledge, biography, and epistemology. Her own experience became her sociological laboratory in many ways, as she explored questions relating to the socialization of children, education, religion, work, social problems, and scientific understanding. She wanted to break down the separation of the private and public spheres, of experience and politics.

139

Martineau was "writing her life" in *Household Education, Life in The Sick Room, Society in America, The Crofton Boys, Letters on the Laws of Man's Nature and Development,* and many of her essays. She had "the special knowledge of the outcast" as Mitzi Myers observes (Myers 1980a, 67). Her wide-ranging and seemingly disparate writings, when examined in relation to her personal experience and intellectual development, reflect a spectrum of concerns. Although one might be tempted to see Martineau's work as the result of a variety of writing opportunities which occurred rather fortuitously over a lifetime, such a view misses the intentionality in her work as she searched for answers and resolutions to societal issues.

Her *Autobiography* can be seen as one of her many studies by this historian-social scientist-educator-journalist. She divided her own two volumes (the third was compiled by Chapman) into six periods which approximated the stages in her intellectual and personal development, the passages through which she travelled, each bringing its own trials, labor and growth. She interpreted her own life against the progressive development of society and of the mind suggested by Condorcet, Saint-Simon, and Auguste Comte in the Law of Three Stages. Not only Western intellectual and cultural history, but also her own intellectual position, she believed, had evolved from theology to philosophy and finally to science. She could understand her own journey best as it, like the history of civilization, reflected the general laws of progress, the natural laws comprising the foundation of all order – natural, social, intellectual.

Notes

1. At the time of her first severe illness in the 1840s friends raised a testimonial fund of £1,400, which provided an annuity that she thought would carry her to her death (*Auto.*, 2:180–81). When, in the late 1860s, her investments in the Brighton Railway ceased bringing in dividends, she had to arrange other means of income, such as the publication of her biographical pieces which had appeared in the *Daily News.*
2. It is interesting to note that Harriet Martineau was born in the house on Magdalen Street which was the birthplace of Elizabeth

Fry, whose work in prison reform she admired. She held in high regard the reformer John Howard, the story of whose life she tried unsuccessfully to publish.

3. Robert K. Webb's "Handlist of Contributions to the *Daily News* by Harriet Martineau 1852–66" contains a list of these leaders. For good summaries of Martineau's journalism, see Pichanick, Chapter VIII, and Webb 1960, Chapter XI.

4. A major movement for domestic reform in the United States in the late nineteenth century, led by such women as Melusina Peirce, Victoria Woodhull, Mary Livermore, Ellen Swallow Richards, and, later, Charlotte Perkins Gilman, worked for kitchenless homes, cooperative housekeeping, cooked food services, and other changes to emancipate women from domestic burdens. An excellent account is given in Dolores Hayden's *The Grand Domestic Revolution: A History of Feminist Designs for American Homes, Neighborhoods, and Cities*, (Cambridge, Massachusetts), 1981.

5. Martineau had, of course, brought many of the current social issues concerning women, science, crime, education, politics, and so forth, to the attention of the public well before the founding of the Association. For a good brief description of the NAPSS and women, see Kathleen E. McCrone, "The National Association for the Promotion of Social Science and the Advancement of Victorian Women, *Atlantis*, Vol. 8, No. 1, Autumn 1982, 44–66. Among the founders and active members were Lord John Russell, Lord Shaftesbury, John Stuart Mill, James Kay-Shuttleworth, Edwin Chadwick, Emily Taylor, Mrs. John Taylor, Barbara Bodichon, Mary Carpenter, Emily Davies, Jessie Boucherett and Mrs. Westlack. McCrone points out the benefits which the Association provided for women, such as contacts with one another, experience in self-assertion and presentation of ideas, and in organization, recruitment to women's causes, and opportunities for the formation of other organizations for women.

6. In the interest of authenticity and of her health, Martineau chose not to change the sketches selected for the volume. A fourth, enlarged edition, containing four additional sketches and her own obituary, written 21 years earlier, appeared in August 1876, two months after her death. The four obituaries were written in the 1870s, including one on Mrs. Somerville, who died in late November 1875. Martineau was writing of others' demise nearly up to the time of her own.

7. This view of history and culture is exemplified in her *History of England* and in articles such as the "Representative Men" series in *Once a Week*.

7 After the Harvest

I am truly grateful to you for taking charge of the chair which I have worked in hope of its bringing in some money – more money than I could offer in any other form – towards obtaining the repeal of the Contagious Diseases Acts. I assure you very earnestly that no one can be more thoroughly aware than I am that this is the very lowest method of assisting the movement . . . in my state of health, no other is open to me. While you and your brave sisters in the enterprise have been enduring exhausting toils, and facing the gravest risks that can appall the matronage and maidenhood of our country, I have been content to ply my needle when I could do no better, and thankful to witness the achievements of the younger and stronger who will live to rejoice in the retrieval of their dear nation.

It was no dream that I indulged in over my work. Nearly forty years ago I saw and felt the first stir, – saw the first steps taken in the wrong direction to suppress the evils of prostitution. After a long enforced pause the attempt was renewed eight years ago, and with a success which saddened a multitude of hearts beside my own. That triumph of wrong and ignorance has clouded the lives of some of the best men and women of England since 1864; but I have seen, for months past, from my easy chair, as I looked abroad over your field of action, the foul vapours dispersed before the strong breeze of the popular opinion and will . . .

—Letter from Martineau to Mrs. Butler, 1871

It is common to picture Harriet Martineau in the period from the mid-1860s until her death in 1876 as an inactive, rather isolated invalid concerned with the miseries of old age and withdrawn from the world and its issues and problems. Such a picture is far from the truth. Certainly she suffered from increasing physical ailments and pain, related to a uterine tumor,

142

hemorrhages, a facial tic, and increased heart strain. While it is true, as evidenced in Martineau's correspondence, that she was less able to write at her previous pace and consequently terminated most of her long-standing obligations, with the *Daily News* for instance, she continued to be engaged in the affairs of society. This is seen most dramatically in her participation in the campaign against the Contagious Diseases Acts 1864–69.

The Contagious Diseases Acts Campaign

Martineau's concerns about women's relationships with men included the issues of prostitution and the sexual exploitation of women. Maria Chapman indicates that in her Tynemouth journal of the early 1840s, Martineau "records the strong feeling that moved her to the service of unhappy women and her conviction that it must be, if possible, a part of her future life" (*Auto.*, 3:427). A sanitary commission established under King William IV had consulted Martineau on the issue of prostitution, but the matter was not pursued further under Queen Victoria until the press made it a *cause celebre* in 1859. At that time Martineau responded with several leaders in the *Daily News* about the need to improve army hygiene and to fight against the sentiment, generated by the press, to control venereal disease among soldiers by implementing laws directed toward women.

The Times gave its support to such laws, and in 1864 Parliament passed the first of three Contagious Diseases Acts. The Act of 1864 concerned eleven military stations and towns and called for the medical examination of prostitutes suspected of being diseased, their detention in hospital if so, and punishment of those brothel owners who kept diseased prostitutes. The second Act, 1866, repealed the first but reinstituted the examination of women in stricter terms, this time providing for periodical examinations for *all* prostitutes and detention of those found to be diseased, without order of a magistrate. The Act of 1869 extended the terms of its predecessor, including more towns and encouraging the examination of any woman suspected of being a prostitute.[1] These acts clearly violated the civil rights of women and made all women, even wives of military men, subject to forced examination and detention. The double standard was in full swing as women were made totally responsible for the sexual health and hygiene of men, according to laws passed by men in Parliament, in each case without notice, opposition, or debate.

Martineau opposed state regulation of prostitution and argued that any such regulation violates the civil rights of men as well as women. In the last days of 1869 she wrote several strong letters to the *Daily News* against the Acts.

> It was sickening to think of such a work; but who should do it if not an old woman, dying and in seclusion . . . I felt that I should have no more peace of mind if I did not obey 'the inward witness' (Letter to Maria Chapman, 30 December 1869).

The letters, signed "An Englishwoman," contained historical background to the measures and criticized in strongest terms those clergy, professions, and people of all classes who complacently misunderstood and naively supported these measures. Martineau charged that some legislators supposed that the acts had to do with cattle rather than people. Most importantly, she became the spokeswoman for the Ladies' National Association for the Repeal of the Contagious Diseases Acts, which she helped to found in 1869, and whose declaration she wrote and published as her fourth item on the Acts, in December 1869 issues of the *Daily News*. Likening the protest by women to these laws, harmful to all women and therefore to the family itself, to Godiva's protest against unfair taxation of the poor, Martineau underscored the victimization of women by these laws:

> Up to the date of the passage of these Bills every woman in the country had the same rights as men over her own person; and the law extended its protection over all alike – of both sexes, and altogether without regard to any question of character, manners, and calling. Prostitutes were as other women, and as men, in their claims upon the law. Now it is no longer. Any woman of whom a policeman swears that he has reason to believe that she is a prostitute is helpless in the hands of the administrators of the new law. She is subject to the extremity of outrage under the eyes, hands, and instruments of surgeons, for the protection of the sex which is the cause of the sin, which is to be protected in further indulgence in it,

and which is passed over by the law, while the victim is punished . . . the legal position of women has been deprived of its most essential security (Martineau, *Daily News*, December 29, 1869, 4).

Martineau emphasized that the problem was the patriarchal control of women by men, the double standard, and the consequent subjection of women:

The Matronage of England protest . . . against the selfishness and cowardness of men . . . being brought to bear upon ruined women [who are] . . . made to endure sufferings inconceivable or incredible by men, in order to enable men to indulge in license with the least risk of incurring any suffering at all (ibid.).

Such legislation, she wrote, far from correcting the negative effects of prostitution, furthers the exploitation of women by England's sons.

In the third letter Martineau argued that such measures simply did not work; they did not check the spread of disease. She included statistics to prove that higher rates of disease occurred in "protected" (by these laws) stations. Indeed, she showed that comparisons of England with France and Belgium bore out the sociologically expected consequences, that legal regulation is associated with higher rather than lower rates of prostitution and disease, since in those circumstances men assume that the state protects them and even condones their use of prostitutes and its consequences. Pointing out the double standard assumed for men in the military as opposed to civilian men, she was critical of the underlying assumption that the former are "necessarily vicious in their propensities if they remain unmarried up to the age of thirty, while no such supposition exists in regard to men of other callings (Martineau, *Daily News*, December 30, 1869, 4). She once again blamed the press for advocating the system and stood firm that "we cannot, will not, must not, surrender any of the personal liberty which is our birthright."

Her letters in the *Daily News* were followed on 31 December 1869, by the Declaration of the Ladies' National Association for the Repeal of the Contagious Diseases Acts, an organization which Martineau described as

145

an association [which] now exists to which my countrywomen may resort for companionship in effort, for information and guidance, and for strengthening in the determination to stand by the personal liberties of every one of us, as we would sustain the honour and life of our country and people (ibid.).

The declaration drawn up by Martineau contained her signature followed by those of Florence Nightingale, Josephine E. Butler, Elizabeth Pease Nichol, Mary Estlin – 128 names in all. Martineau's letters and the declaration were reprinted in a pamphlet for the Association. She contributed to petitions for formation of groups and meetings on the cause, to speeches, and to letters to politicians and citizens, especially to efforts against politicians who supported this legislation. In the campaign for reelection of Sir Henry Storks, an outspoken advocate of the Contagious Diseases Acts, a strong effort by Martineau and others directed toward the women of Colchester resulted in his defeat. The following placard was used in other similar circumstances, as these women realized the necessity of strong political action to accomplish their goal of abolition:

Old England!
Purity and Freedom!

To the Electors of North Nottinghamshire

We, as Englishwomen, loving our country and our old National Constitution, entreat you, the Electors of North Nottinghamshire, in the name of Religion, of Morality, and of our National Freedom, to vote for no man who will not pledge himself to vote for the total and unconditional Repeal of those un-English Laws, that Continental abomination stealthily smuggled into our Statute-Book, called the Contagious Diseases Acts, and to oppose any Future Legislation that involves their Principles.

Harriet Martineau
Josephine Butler
Ursula Bright
Lydia E. Becker

In 1871 Harriet wrote to a friend:

> The conspiracy of silence is broken up, and the London papers have burst out. Our main point now is, to secure every variety of judgment inside and outside of the Commission. The 'Daily News' came out clearly and strongly on the right side before any other London paper broke the silence. The satisfaction to us all is immense, to see the paper uphold its high character – the very highest – in this hour of crisis. I feel unusually ill in consequence of heart-failure, but I must make you know something of what you shall know more of hereafter (Reprinted in Chapman's *Memorials, Auto.*, 3:435).

The report of a Royal Commission in 1871, which recommended a return to the Act of 1864 whereby only prostitutes suspected of being diseased be examined, was not implemented. Josephine Butler was encouraged by Martineau and others to lead the campaign against the Acts. The dedicated efforts of individuals such as Butler, and James Stansfeld in the house of Commons, led finally to suspension of the Acts in 1883 and their ultimate repeal in 1886 (Rover, 78–81).

Butler, more interested in issues on education, advocated "voluntary self-control," and maintained that the elimination of vice and disease is a moral question – "health will follow upon morality." Nonetheless, Butler was also changed by her own participation in the campaign against the Acts. She played an important role in the International Association for Moral and Social Hygiene, advocated abolition of state regulation of vice, worked to rescue prostitutes from exploitation and abuse, and remained active in the cause until 1901.

During this period of increasing age and illness, Martineau, with the aid of her niece Maria, second daughter of Robert and Jane, and the other women of the household, continued to follow contemporary events and to write letters and articles when she felt it necessary or desirable. Maria, with whom she had been very close and on whom she depended a great deal, died of typhoid in 1864. Her death was a terrible loss for Harriet; Maria's sister Jane took her place. Around 1873 Jenny, as she was called, as well as Caroline the maid, became ill, and both had to leave the Knoll. They were replaced by the cook Marianne and a young woman by the name of Una Goodwin.

In spite of these losses and physical problems, Martineau, helped by her companions, still frequently wrote ten- to twelve-page letters to politicians and friends to give her opinions and analysis on a myriad of topics. Her health steadily declined; she had periods when descending the stairs and even breathing with ease became nearly impossible. Her resistance to full physical examination was probably due to a fear of surgery.

Despite illness and old age, Martineau was not forgotten by her friends and colleagues and the British public. In 1873 Monckton Milnes (Lord Houghton), in his presidential address at the Social Science Congress in Norwich, paid tribute "to the woman whose name must always be associated with the city" (Wheatley, 384).

Although in the 1870s Martineau had to refuse requests to write on certain subjects and to take on new work because of her weakening state, she remained actively concerned about the welfare of people, especially the disadvantaged, the treatment of women and children, obstacles to economic equity, and the resistance of institutions which worked against natural liberties. Martineau "in her own way, and according to her lights . . . played the part of a national conscience" (Pichanick: 200–37) long after she discontinued her regular participation in the affairs of the nation.[2]

Salem Witchcraft

In 1868 Martineau stepped out of her retirement to publish an article on "Salem Witchcraft," a review of Charles Upham's 1867 publication on the subject which had been sent to her from America.[3] She wrote to her cousin Henry Reeve, who was editor of the *Edinburgh Review*. "What would you think of my trying to do this one more bit of work?" Martineau still approached her work with thoroughness; the review ran thirty-one pages. Her fascination with American history and society is exceeded in this article only by her interest in the analysis of so-called witchcraft and the consequent hysteria in Salem, Massachusetts, in particular.

Martineau wrote in her usual straight-forward manner. Her copy of the galley proofs of the article with her own minor alterations and additions, dated April 27 1868, was returned to the Review where subsequent changes and cuts were made to the text without her knowledge or permission prior to publication. She later obtained the proofs and noted the publisher's unauthorized changes on those pages. She wrote a number of letters of complaint and clarification to Reeve to correct the distortions in meaning which she felt had resulted. In the quotes which follow the publisher's changes are indicated.

Drawing on Upham's text she presented the sociological setting of Salem, a community of originally largely landed aristocracy, whose conflicts with artisans and others over the division of land preceded the campaign against witches. She analyzed the politics and religion which incited the passion of "Indian-hating" and the view of Indians as agents of Satan. In her view, conflicts among economic groups and discord over church authority and gerontocratic rule were responsible for the stir of suspicion and punitiveness of citizens toward one another.

Religious ideology in Salem was based to considerable extent on superstition and factious notions declaring a war against Satan and establishing Satanic evidence and condemnation wherever convenience or helplessness allowed. The clergy were important parties to it all. Reflecting her theory on the history of ideas and society, Martineau concluded that this was an unfortunate consequence of the theological period of a society:

> In [our day] it [Deodat Lawson's sermon on the devil] is an instructive evidence of the extent to which 'knowledge falsely so called' may operate on the mind of society, in the absence of science and before the time has arrived for a clear understanding of the nature of knowledge and the conditions of its attainment (HM, "Salem Witchcraft," *Edinburgh Review*, July 1868:13).

Martineau pointed out

> that the generation concerned had no alternative explanation within their reach, when perplexed by unusual appearances or actions of body or mind. They believed themselves perfectly certain about the Devil and his doings . . . The very conception of science had then scarcely begun to be formed in the minds of the wisest men of the time (ibid., 14).

149

Martineau's interpretation of events is based on her hypothesis that the Salem witch hunt resulted from inadequate knowledge of the relations of body and mind. By this she meant, not only that ignorance buttressed by theology prevailed in the absence of scientific understanding, but also that spiritualist or so-called lunatic behavior was seen by Salem citizens as the Devil's work, rather than as psychophysical phenomena which could be scientifically accounted for.[4]

> Those [of us] who have given due and dispassionate attention to the processes of mesmerism and their effects can have no difficulty in understanding the reports handed down of what these young creatures did, and said, and saw, under peculiar conditions of the nervous system (ibid., 18).

Martineau's review of Upham's work demonstrates her sociological and feminist understanding – sociological, in showing the social attribution of character, social control and the spread of social hysteria in the community, and the insidious role of authority; feminist, in revealing and condemning the public's association of women with evil, the exertion of male power over women, and the suffering which women in particular, if not solely, endured. As for the strange powers or faculties as well as nervous disturbances of some of the Salem victims, Martineau maintained that the possibility of the phenomenon of somnambulism, or hypnotic-like states, could account for many of these incidents and criticized Upham's inability or unwillingness to recognize it.

> It is impossible to witness these phenomena [the curious phenomena of somnambulism and catalepsy] without a keen sense of how natural and even inevitable it was for *the mesmeric* subjects of the Middle Ages & of Puritan times to believe themselves ensnared by Satan, & actually endowed with his gifts, & to confess their calamity, as the only relief to their scared & miserable minds. This explanation seems not to have occurred to Mr. Upham; & for want of it, he falls into great amazement at the elaborate artifice with which the sufferers invented their confessions, & adapted them to the state of mind of the authorities & the public. With the right key in his hand, he would have seen only what was simple and natural where he now bids us marvel at the pitch of artfulness & skill attained by poor wretches scared out of their natural wits

(ibid., 35; pages 23–24 of proofs. Added to the proofs by Martineau's hand. Material in brackets added and italicized words omitted by publisher from final text).

Martineau was convinced that the "fetish tendency" became reaffirmed in society – "that constant tendency to explain everything by the facts, the feelings, and the experience of the individual's own nature," that is, the unwillingness to explore reasonably rather than condemn and punish:

> We may believe that we could never act as the citizens of Salem acted in their superstition and their fear; and this may be true, *though there are signs of willingness to be as cruel to those who perplex us as our witch-hunting forefathers ever were,* but *our* course of speculation is, in *our* 'spiritual circles', very much the same as in Mr Parris' parlour (ibid., 42; 27 in proofs. Italicized material omitted by publisher in final text).

Martineau recognized the early stage in which we find ourselves in the explanation of the

> well-known and indisputable facts which occur from time to time. . . . such facts as the phenomena of [natural] somnambulism, *of seeing without eyes,* of double consciousness, of suspended sensation while consciousness is awake . . . of a wide range of intellectual and instinctive operations bearing the character of marvels to such as cannot wait for the solution (italicized words omitted by publisher; word in brackets added; ibid.).

She continues:

> We are still far from being able to explain such mysteries, in the only true sense of the word *explaining* – that is, being able to refer the facts to the natural *law* [cause] to which they belong; but we have an incalculable advantage over people of former centuries in knowing that for all proved facts there is a *law* [natural cause]; that every *law* [cause] to which proved facts within our cognisance are attached is destined to become known to us; and that, in the present case, we have learned in what direction to search for it, and have set out on *our* [the] quest. *Of course,* none of us can offer even the remotest conjecture as to what the law of the common action of what we call mind and body may be. If we could, the

discovery would have been already made. But, instead of necessarily assuming, as the Salem people did, that what they witnessed was the operation of spiritual upon human beings, we have, as our field of observation and study, a region undreamed of by them – the brain as an organised part of the human frame, and the nervous system, implicating more facts, more secrets, and more marvels than our forefathers attributed to the whole body (ibid.).

The publisher had substituted cause or natural cause for law, as shown, and thereby changed the meaning, as Martineau protested in her letter to Henry Reeve. She meant law in the sense of *general fact*

> to which special facts may be referred, by which facts from a wide range of observation are classified, that reference and classification constituting *explanation* in its philosophical sense. In this sense the province of Law is *Science*, and its field is the whole range of natural phenomena. It has no cognizance of *Cause* (Letter by Martineau to Henry Reeve, 7 August 1868).

She goes on to complain that the publisher's changes rendered the text "not only faulty but unintelligible."

> "Gravitation" is called a "law," not because any idea of Will or decree comes into it, but because it is the *General Fact* to which a multitude of special facts, from all parts of the universe, never before suspected to have any connexion, must be referred, – that reference, once established, constituting the "explanation" of them. No question of the *nature* of the force concerned, nor of the *cause* of the phenomena, enters into the inquiry at all (ibid.).

Martineau, the Baconian rationalist, was more convinced than ever that science would lead to our understanding of the mysteries of life. The positivism which she had expounded in the previous decade remained an important part of her epistemology.

> Amidst the conflict of phenomena of the human mind and body, we have arrived now at the express controversy of Psychology against Physiology . . . The first cannot be, with any

152

accuracy, called a science at all, and the other is in little more than a rudimentary state . . . while there is still a multitude deluding and disporting itself with a false hypothesis about certain mysteries of the human mind, and claiming to have explained the marvels of Spiritualism by making an objective world of their own subjective experience, the scientific physiologists are proceeding, by observation and experiment, to penetrate more and more secrets of our intellectual and moral life ("Salem Witchcraft": 47).

Here the article ends. But, as the proofs of 27 April 1868 show, nearly three pages of text were omitted from the final copy. In the passages cut by the publisher, Martineau draws attention to the fact that many mysteries of the mind-thought, perception, consciousness and unconsciousness – remain unaccounted for. She points out that there are many hospitals in Europe using mesmeric treatments for diseases, but that they are unfortunately ignored by the medical and scientific professions. "Some of the spirit of the clerical, medical, and judicial bigots of Salem survives in our generation." Clearly, the publisher's decision to omit her criticisms indicates their desire to avoid the controversy over mesmerism and her tenacious support of it, and perhaps her critique of the medical establishment. She, on the other hand, was very interested in the frontiers of knowledge and the unexplored region of psychology.

Martineau's perspective in this last periodical piece, and perhaps her motive for writing it, is a reaffirmation of her commitment to rationalism and to science as the way toward the good society. It reasserts her rejection of prejudice and narrowness and her advocacy of tolerance, openness and reason. Finally, it provided an opportunity for her to reaffirm her support for mesmerism and somnambulism as means to understand and treat the medical complications of mind and body.

She remained an important figure. Reeve had acceded to her request to do this particular piece, and hers was the lead article in that issue of the Review. She remained as well a woman of controversial views, which, even in this instance, were not given a complete hearing.

The Last Project

When Una Goodwin, Martineau's new aid, began the translation of Reinhold Pauli's *Simon de Montfort*, an historical biography of the creator of the House of Commons, she learned that her prospective publisher wanted Martineau to write an introduction. Martineau agreed and wrote the Introduction, her last piece of work for publication, in spring 1876 (Wheatley, 386). Evidently, Martineau's sponsorship remained important to any publisher. The Introduction is the omega, her reminder of the significance of understanding history through biography – "the interest and efficacy of the study of History itself, by the road of Biography," as she put it.

> It is not merely that human character is always and everywhere supremely interesting to meditative men; it is that in a man's life we see his mind; and that the more we see of his life the better we understand his mind, and can interpret his ideas, designs, and acts.[5]

The work was, in fact, a new edition, having been revised by Pauli and translated from the German by Una Goodwin. Martineau was happy to have a part in the establishment of Montfort's place in history, which she felt had long suffered from neglect. His contribution of the "extension of political function to the Commons and the principle of Representation" exemplified his great character and his appreciation of the people. This new political biography would set history right and "secure his name and fame from neglect and perversion."

> Under the remarkable development of Historical study at present, as the education of both sexes receives extension, this work will surely be welcomed for any one of its several bearings; and among them all there will scarcely be room left for any generation henceforth to ask, as our grandfathers too often did – "Was Simon de Montfort a great and good man?"
> H.M. May, 1876

Notes

1. See Constance Rover, *Love, Morals and the Feminists*, London: Routledge & Kegan Paul, 1970, especially Chapter nine.
2. During this period she once again refused the (Gladstone) Government's offer of a pension. She had always maintained that accepting such a pension might curtail her ability to be absolutely free to criticize government policies. In fact, she saw such assistance as a threat to her hard-won financial independence.
3. Charles W. Upham, *Salem Witchcraft; with an Account of Salem Village, and a History of Opinions on Witchcraft and Kindred Subjects*, 2 vols. (Boston, 1867).
4. Using Upham's text Martineau identified the psychological phenomena of projection and scapegoating engendered by the insecurities of life in the New World. Like other sociological positivists of her time, and considerably before Freud, Martineau analyzed the psychological motivations underlying social behavior in many of her writings.
5. Introduction, Reinhold Pauli, *Simon de Montfort, Earl of Leicester, The Creator of the House of Commons*, translated by Una M. Goodwin, (London: Trubner & Co., Ludgate Hill, 1876), iv.

8 A Woman of Principle

> If half the thought and sentiment that are spent on the subject of Death were bestowed on the practical duty of strengthening, lengthening, and ennobling Life, we should be more fit to live worthily, and die contentedly. Let us prepare the way for the next generation.
> —Harriet Martineau, *Health, Husbandry, and Handicraft*, 1861

> We find ourselves suddenly living and moving in the midst of the universe — as a part of it, and not as its aim and object. We find ourselves living, not under capricious and arbitrary conditions, unconnected with the constitution and movements of the whole. Certainly, I can conceive of no instruction so favorable to aspiration as that which shows us how great are our faculties, how small our knowledge, how sublime the heights which we may hope to attain, and how boundless an infinity may be assumed to spread beyond.
> —Harriet Martineau, "Preface" to her translation of Comte's *Positive Philosophy*, 1853

The old woman finally succumbed to old age and illness, her state made increasingly difficult by news of the deaths of friends and colleagues. Restricting herself to her bedroom by early June of 1876, she arose each day, dressed and sat by her window to gaze upon the world from the Knoll, as she had done so many times. Later in the month she developed bronchitis, which consumed her strength, and soon she was too weak to leave her bed. As the sun was setting in Ambleside on 27 June 1876 Harriet Martineau quietly submitted to death.

Martineau, who had always maintained that no church would wish to harbor her bones in its graveyard, was convinced in her last days by her relatives to consent to burial in Birmingham. Her name, identification, and dates were added to the gravestone in Key Cemetery bearing the same for her parents, and Robert, wife Jane, and Maria. She probably would have preferred the Lake District. Martineau's burial place was a source of controversy even before her death. Writer and editor James Payn relates that

> there was even some correspondence in the local paper as to the impropriety of her being buried in the churchyard, which was, to say the least of it, premature. 'I suggest the quarry', she once said to me with a humorous twinkle of her kind eyes; 'but Mr. Atkinson says that I should spoil the quarry'. She was too used to unpopularity to be disturbed by it (Payn, 113–14).

Martineau's attitude toward death, upon which she had much occasion to reflect, was continuous with her view of human life and its humble place in the universe. She wrote in 1844:

> Thus, we grieve, and cannot but grieve, at the death of a friend, whose absence will leave a blank in our life: but the laying down our own life, to yield our place to our successors, and simply ceasing to be, seems to me to admit of no fear or regret, except through the corruption introduced by false and superstitious associations (*Auto.*, 2:206).

Death, like life, afforded certain opportunities. Martineau had decided twenty years earlier to serve society in death by willing her head to science. Her interest in phrenology and mesmerism had promoted the decision, which she left to Henry Atkinson to carry out. He did not fulfill her request, however.

A story is told by James Payn that Martineau decided at one point to bequeath her ears to a Dr. Toynbee, a London otologist, because he had been so kind her in consultation. Her own doctor Shepherd, upon learning of that, said: "But, my dear madam, you can't do that; it will make your other legacy worthless." When Payn inquired as to how he knew it, the doctor replied, "Oh, she told me so herself; she has left ten pounds in her codicil to me for cutting it off" (Payn, 126–27).

Martineau defined death as simply an event of life at which one's deed and contributions could be assessed, the meaning of a life identified. And so, in assessing Martineau's own life, we could not begin at a more appropriate place than her own obituary, her "Autobiographic Memoir" (see also Chapter 6).

157

Written long before, the obituary was published in the *Daily News* on 29 June 1876. Fully aware of Martineau's standards for herself as well as others, the *Daily News* prefaced her "self-estimate" thus: "The frankness of its self-criticism makes it necessary to guard the reader against confounding her own strict and sometimes disparaging judgment of herself with the impressions made by her upon others." The memoir epitomizes in many respects the life of Harriet Martineau as the pursuit of clarification, demystification, and stark honesty.

In describing the evolution of her own writing career, beginning with religious works and moving on to political economy, she explained her motivation: "Her stimulus in all she wrote, from first to last, was simply the need of utterance." Citing her tales in political economy as, not only the successful onset of her writing career but exemplary of the duty she especially felt towards the working classes in society, she wrote:

> The original idea of exhibiting the great natural laws of society by a series of pictures of selected social action was a fortunate one; and her tales initiated a multitude of minds into the conception of what political economy is, and of how it concerns every body living in society. Beyond this, there is no merit of a high order in the work. It did not pretend to offer discoveries, or new applications or elucidations of prior discoveries. It popularised, in a fresh form, some doctrines and many truths long before made public by others (Obituary, *Auto.*, 3:461–62).

She saw her own fiction as having no permanent character, and admitted that she nearly ceased writing fiction "from simple inability to do it well." Martineau's judgment is harsher than those of her contemporaries, such as George Eliot, Elizabeth Gaskell, and Charlotte Brontë, all of whom, in fact, were impressed by *Deerbrook* and regarded it as a model for some of their own works (Sanders 1986, xi, et passim).

Martineau's obituary emphasized particularly her historical and sociological writings, specifically the America books, *Eastern Life* (one of her favorites), *Letters on the Laws of Man's Nature and Development*, *Household Education*, and the condensation of Comte's *Positive Philosophy*. Of the latter she said "it was her last considerable work; and *there is no other, perhaps, which so well manifests the real character of her ability and proper direction of her influence"* (ibid.: 469. Emphasis added.). This is an indication of Martineau's lasting identification with the positive science of society and of her desire to be remembered as a contributor to the new sociological understanding of reality. However, her view of her own work was modest and candid:

> Her original power was nothing more than was due to earnestness and intellectual clearness within a certain range. With small imaginative and suggestive powers, and therefore nothing approaching to genius, she could see clearly what she did see, and give clear expression to what she had to say. In short, she could popularize, while she could neither discover nor invent. She could sympathize in other people's views, and was too facile in doing so; and she could obtain and keep a firm grasp of her own, and, moreover, she could make them understood . . . She saw the human race, as she believed, advancing under the law of progress; she enjoyed her share of the experience, and had no ambition for a large endowment, or reluctance or anxiety about leaving the enjoyment of such as she had (ibid.: 469–70).

The View of Others

One is always struck, in the matter of history's assessment of Harriet Martineau, by the controversy, the variety of opinions, and the ambivalence of those who knew her. She was part of a generation of Victorian intellectuals, writers, politicians, artists, and professionals who were trying to come to terms with the impact of modernity on British society still imbued with traditionalism. They were engaged by, and passionate about, complex and controversial issues concerning education, industrialization, business and economic policy, political participation, social reform and the impact of science. The recognition of the eclipse of the traditional world and the anxiety produced by the uncertainties of the modern world resulted in ambivalence, fears, and contradictions in the Victorian mind, as Walter Houghton has shown in considerable detail. Anxiety accompanied optimism, as the critical spirit and religious doubt haunted the will to believe. Rigidity and an entrepreneurial

159

anti-intellectualism went along with enthusiasm for change and progressive idealism (see Houghton).

Harriet Martineau was every bit as contradictory and complex, persevering and uncertain, dogmatic and humane as others of her generation. For example, in reflecting a decade later on the writing of *Life in the Sickroom*, she recognized her own incertitude and admitted that she "was unconsciously trying to gain strength of conviction by vigour of assertion" (*Auto.*, 2:187). And we recall that Martineau's 1851 invocation of the timely importance of Comte's positive philosophy emphasized that it was a needed intellectual solution to the uncertainties of the age. But this period of uncertainty was also one of exploration and experimentation, many instances of which we can see in Martineau and her generation.

Harriet Martineau's personality, her views, and the expanse of her writings created a great variety of reactions. She had many friends. These included Lord and Lady Durham, the Carlyles, Malthuses, Arnolds, Follens, Garrison, Elisabeth Reid, Lady Byron, Lady Elgin, Julia Smith, Maria Chapman, Elizabeth Browning, Charlotte Brontë, George Eliot, Henry Crabb Robinson, William J. Fox, Monckton-Milnes, Charles and, especially, Erasmus Darwin, and of course Henry George Atkinson, her closest friend and confidant for the last third of her life, whose bust "decorated her study and inspired her labours throughout her later life" (Bosanquet, 157). Many of her friendships endured and prospered; some were terminated or damaged by Martineau's sense of propriety – for example, concerning the extramarital relationships of Eliot and Lewes, and J. S. Mill and Harriet Hardy Taylor – or by Martineau's own views on social issues, as in her disagreement with Margaret Fuller over slavery.

She was read and consulted by many in government and diplomacy, lord chancellors, chancellors of the exchequer, cabinet ministers, members of parliament, and foreign dignitaries. Her help was enlisted to promote government policy through her writings. She was asked by Sweden to act as a consultant on political constitutions. The Italians wanted her to study their political status vis-à-vis Austria. O'Connell wanted her to study Irish affairs and to report to that country and England (*Auto.*, 2:311–12, 315). She was asked at least twice to edit new journals in the field of economics.

The times were ripe for just such a mind and powers as hers. There were flagrant and irrational abuses in politics and law and the social economy of the nation. No one could clearly and honestly defend the abuses in the representative system. . . . the horrors of the penal code . . . the heavy import duties on corn . . .This was the order of problem to which Harriet Martineau devoted her powers of clear perception and expression in the heyday of her fame (Marvin, 633–34).

Florence Nightingale saw Martineau as a devoted and indeed devout woman, as well as a champion of human rights and justice.

She was born to be a destroyer of slavery, in whatever form, in whatever place, all over the world, wherever she saw or thought she saw it. The thought actually inspired her: whether in the degraded offspring of former English poor-law, of English serfdom forty years ago, – in any shape; whether in the fruits of any abuse, – social, legislative, or administrative, – or in actual slavery; or be it in Contagious Diseases Acts, or no matter what, she rose to the occasion. I think, contradictory as it may seem, she had the truest and deepest religious feeling I have ever known (*Auto.*, 3:479–80).

Nightingale continued to think of Martineau as a Christian and reflected the view of many of Martineau's friends and acquaintances who refused to accept her frank and clear agnosticism. Of course Martineau never denied first Cause but thought it to be beyond human knowledge and understanding.

Upon her death most commentators singled out some element of her personality and life's work which helped to compose the mosaic of her accomplishment and her influence. James Payn, for example, wrote to Jane Martineau: "I have known all the famous women of our own time, or about all, and I think that, taking her character all around, your aunt *was* the greatest among them." He commented on her "motherliness" and her "keen sense of fun" and remarked on the relation of her character to her physical disabilities:

This deprivation of the external senses may have had considerable influence in forming Miss Martineau's mental characteristics; but if it turned her attention to studies more or less

161

abstruse, and which are seldom pursued by those of her own sex, it certainly never 'hardened' her (Payn 1884, 118–19).

Elsewhere Payn drew a positive and rather accurate picture of Martineau:

> She was, no doubt, somewhat masterful in argument, but I always found her very ready to listen, and especially to any tale of woe or hardship which it lay in her power to remedy . . . Rarely have I know a social companion more bright and cheery . . . She had known more interesting and eminent persons than most men, and certainly than any woman of her time; the immense range of her writings, political, religious, and social, had caused her to make acquaintance with people of the most different opinions and of all ranks, while amongst the large circle of her personal acquaintance, her motherly qualities, her gentleness, and (on delicate domestic questions) her good judgment, made her the confidant of many persons, especially young people . . . I never knew a woman whose nature was more essentially womanly than that of Harriet Martineau (ibid., 112–13).

In the obituary for Bradlaugh's *National Reformer*, George Holyoake, a dear friend of Harriet, also commented on Martineau's "womanly" character: "Like most women of thought, as she grew old, she grew more beautiful. Later in life, she had quite a queenly look" (cited in Wheatley, 388).

Matthew Arnold praised her in poetry following her translation of Comte, and perhaps more than any other contemporary seemed to understand her religious and philosophical voyage and the inevitable changes in her ideas and beliefs.

The assessments of Martineau and her work were not unmixed; she had been fully aware of that. As Vera Wheatley has suggested, many confused her self-confidence with vanity and her advanced opinions with dogmatism. Thomas Carlyle gave a rather churlish assessment:

> To admire her literary genius, or even her solidity of common sense, was never possible for either of us: but she had a sharp eye, an imperturbable self-possession, and in all things a swiftness of positive decision, which, joined to her evident loyalty of intention, and her frank, guileless, easy ways, we both liked . . . Her talent, which in that sense was very consid-

162

erable, I used to think, would have made her a quite shining Matron of some big Female Establishment, mistress of some immense Dress-Shop, but was totally inadequate to grapple with deep spiritual and social questions, – into which she launched, nothing doubting . . . The 'exchange of ideas' with her was seldom of behoof in our poor sphere. But she was practically very good (Thomas Carlyle, *Reminiscences*: 437–38).

Harriet would have smiled at such estimations, as she undoubtedly did during her life, although sometimes with penetrating hurt. Nonetheless, she was too busy and too committed to what she had defined as her vocation to be restrained by negative opinions of her work or her personality. She certainly saw herself as strong-minded and task-oriented, determined to carry out her work as she saw fit. There is great honesty and truth in her view of her own unsuitability for marriage and family life. Yet, as Henry Richardson points out in *The Contemporary Review*, "in some things she was made for domestic life. The love of home was strong within her. She liked what was quiet and permanent; affections bringing duties, and duties fortifying affections" (Richardson, 1114–15).

W.R. Greg, in reviewing her *Autobiography* in 1877, was concerned that Martineau had given too negative a picture of herself, and, although he labelled her as arrogant and "having convictions of the fanatic and martyr," said that she could not easily have been less dogmatic, less hasty, or less imperious than she was (Wheatley, 392). Regarding her personality, he stressed that, although she gave the impression of being ill-natured and even bitter and depreciatory, she was in fact kind-hearted and affectionate. It is well known that she had a good sense of humor, and that she did not seek sympathy in her illnesses. If she demanded much from others, it was because she demanded a great deal from herself. She was cursed, in some respects, by an exaggerated sense of duty and responsibility to others and to society, which resulted in an apparent conceit and self-righteousness. "She loved much and laboured hard for the happiness of others," Greg concludes. He points to her motivation thus:

She never, after her very youthful years, wrote either for money or for fame. She wrote because the matter was borne in upon her, because the thing in her conception 'wanted saying,' and it was in her to say it . . . The truth is that doubt seems to have been a state of mind unknown to her. She never *reconsidered* her opinions, or mused over her judgments (Greg, 1882, 184).

Martineau's life had taken an entirely different course from that of her theologian-philosopher brother James. Her death precipitated James's public denunciation of his sister's posthumously published version of her family life and relationships, particularly regarding their mother. James defended their mother as having been a kind, caring, and intelligent woman, who most certainly could not be held responsible for Harriet's childhood problems and poor self-esteem. He attributed his sister's peculiarities and antireligious attitudes to her health problems. Alfred Benn has summarized the work and lives of the brother and sister:

> The two Martineaus started from the same ideal basis, and each retained to the end one of the elements into which it split under the stress of a dissolving dialectic. The sister, holding fast to her philosophy of determinism and experience, ultimately became a convert to Positivism. The brother, holding fast to his religion of personal theism, found his way to accepting free will together with as many intuitions as were needed to save the necessity of proving his position – the sort of half-mysticism which is a compromise between reason and tradition. In this instance . . . more fearless consistency is displayed by the woman than by the man (Benn, 2:67).

Martineau, the Sociologist

Martineau undoubtedly had an impact on the thinking and understanding of all classes in British society at the time. Most of all, she had advanced the sociological understanding of a society on the threshold of modernity. Whatever else, Harriet Martineau wanted to understand the implications of the new age and to help others in society to understand them as well. She was a woman of science, of the moral sciences, and particularly sociology – the science of society. It is revealing that she considered her condensation of Comte's *Positive Philosophy*, which introduced French positivism into English thought, to be among all her writings the best reflection of her direction and influence. Beyond that, "for years she had been preaching sociology without the name" (Webb, 1960, 308).

She was indeed a daughter of the Enlightenment. Science was important to her, whether in the area of political economy, the social laws of society, positivist methodology, the creation of new technology to free human beings for higher pursuits, or the study of mind-body relations, suggested by mesmerism and phrenology.

Like Jane Marcet, but to a far greater degree, Martineau wrote works covering an immense range of topics in social science, literature and history. Any examination or criticism of her work must therefore cast its net wide. Other biographies and analyses of Martineau have presented critiques of her work from the perspectives of literature and journalism. In this study we have examined the life and work of Harriet Martineau from the perspective of sociology, and therefore will look briefly at those criticisms of her work which emanate from social scientific figures or circles.

With regard to her writings in political economy, we have already seen their enormous popularity with the general readership (10,000 copies per month by 1834). Mark Blaug reminds us that "almost the entire periodical press, daily, weekly, and monthly, received it with glowing praise. Readers as diverse as Victoria and Coleridge waited anxiously for each new number . . . even the economists were won over, although they had been skeptical" (Blaug 1958, 129–30).

As we have seen, James Mill thought Martineau's approach in combining political economy and fiction bound to fail, and John Stuart Mill saw her efforts as less than satisfactory, although he never was able to evaluate Martineau's work free of their personal antagonisms. Mill said that "Harriet Martineau reduces the laissez-faire system to absurdity by carrying it out in all its consequences" (J.S. Mill to Thomas Carlyle, *Letters of John Stuart Mill*, 1910, 1:46).

But Blaug points out that "actually, there is no ground whatsoever for this opinion and it seems less than fair to condemn her for what is after all a perfectly standard treatment of the proper scope of government" (ibid., 138). She can be seen as perhaps the most popular writer to bring the issues of economy, law, trade, and population together to bear upon the problems in English society at the time and to make such analyses accessible to the general public. Bringing together Ricardian economics and socialist labor theory, she showed the links among the principles of social life and their impact on all classes.

Blaug maintains that Martineau in some respects perpetuated economic ideas, such as Smith's identity of interests and Malthus's population theory which were already being discarded, and therefore helped to delay reception of Ricardian economics. She was familiar with Ricardo's ideas mainly from the writings of Dugald Stewart who subsequently influenced Ricardo (*Auto.*, 1:106). Furthermore, the theories of Smith and Malthus permeated the political economy of the time and appear as late as 1848 in J.S. Mill's *Principles of Political Economy*.[1] Indeed, classical political economy continued to influence economic analysis for some time.

In his book *The Great Transformation*, Karl Polanyi recognized Martineau to have been a major influence in spreading the doctrines of classical political economy and in that sense contributing to the acceleration of British capitalism. Martineau's characterization of capitalism was the liberal version; she worked diligently and successfully to promote the equation of progress, democracy, and capitalism. She is seen as a central figure in the nineteenth-century attempt to "make immediately and practically recognizable principles which were widely thought to be abstract and difficult to understand" (Simon Dentith, 191).

The theme of her work was the Law of Progress, which science alone could help us to understand. Webb, her first academic biographer, comments that her life was astonishingly consistent, based as it was on the pursuit of, and dedication to, the truth. Difficult as it is, within the changing political spectrum in England in the nineteenth century, to define her politics, Webb identifies her as a Radical who subscribed to rationalism, progress, human dignity and equality, human perfectibility, and the infinite possibilities of human understanding (Cf. Webb 1960, especially Chapters III and XII). His thesis, that Martineau's radicalism shares much with that of her contemporary Karl Marx, points to the sociological disposition of both. They shared a strong belief in the emancipatory power of science and rational knowledge. They shared an Enlightenment faith in human capabilities and potentialities, that is, in human perfectibility. They analyzed the consequences of industrialization and capitalism within nineteenth-century society. Both had bourgeois origins and tended to idealize the days of classical "petit bourgeois" economies. Both were concerned with the fate of the working classes, and both believed in the emancipatory potential of industrialization.

Marx concluded that the capitalist system itself was inhumane, alienating, and bound for destruction. Martineau, too, was concerned about the alienating and degrading aspects of industrial work, particularly where women and children were concerned. But her views were rooted in the liberal commercial perspective of the Dissenters. She took a harsh attitude toward the "carelessness" of workers (including children) in using machinery when it resulted in injury and death. She saw class conflict as disruptive to social progress; she was not, however, utopian with respect to the existence of classes. But, like Marx, she did look to the possibilities for community, for human cooperation free of class conflict, and for a society, as she stated in an early essay, where people would contribute according to their abilities and be rewarded according to their contribution (rather than need) – a liberal rather than socialist proposal. As Webb points out, both thinkers had a tenacious faith in science; political economy became the fulcrum for pursuing their respective analyses. They understood the need for a theory with which to understand social reality and to proceed with practical programs. The legacy of Saint-Simon was important for both.

The radicalism of each took a distinct course: Marx became a revolutionary socialist; Martineau became a feminist sociologist. Marx saw the future of society and human emancipation to lie in the political action of the working classes, leading to the abolition of class society. Martineau saw society's future in the equality of women and men, enlightened reform and co-operation among social classes, led by the middle class, and a publicly-shared (insofar as possible) body of knowledge based on the new Moral Sciences. For Marx, the key to historical change was dialectics; for Martineau, it was social evolution, based upon the Law of Three Stages. From different perspectives Marx and Martineau were interested in the advance of society down the road of social progress, and in human development based on a foundation of freedoms and rights of the individual. For Marx, this required the emancipation of the working classes; for Martineau, the emancipation of women and slaves. This is fundamental to her sociology.

The controversy over the evaluation of Martineau's work and contributions results, not only from the scope of her writings and of the issues she dealt with, but also from her location at the center of the major debates, and even battles, of the day. As Noel Annan has shown, "the battle between rationalism and religion was fought by both sides almost entirely on positivist ground." And positivism "began from the individual and moved out toward society" (Annan, 11, 5). Martineau approached the debate with both enthusiasm and reservation about positivism; enthusiasm because positivism as 'the philosophy of fact' vitiated the nihilism of skepticism and provided a positive, optimistic image of human beings and society consistent with her own perspective; reservation because her own experiences and philosophy led her to conclude that what was needed was not a positivist "religion of humanity" but a humane, rational, secular philosophy for living.

How was Martineau regarded by the Comteans? England's best known disciple of Comtean sociology, Frederic Harrison, was sharply critical of Martineau for having excluded, in her translation of Comte, the last pages of *Cours de Philosophie Positive* in which Comte outlines his Religion of Humanity. In an 1896 edition of Martineau's translation of Comte, Harrison restored those pages and added his own introduction. Although he included Comte's praise for Martineau's condensations and translation, he went on to focus on his own objections to her work. Over time, however, Martineau's version of Comte became the standard one, and Harrison's critique was ignored.[2]

We are only now beginning to discover the influence which Harriet Martineau had on subsequent sociologists. Evidence is emerging that her work was read by numerous people whose names became more prominent than hers in sociology in Europe and America. Throughout the twentieth century, sociology developed its progressive mission as a social science and discarded its own history as an anachronism, as a primitive stage in its own inimitable maturation. A renewed focus on, and understanding of, the emergence of sociology in the context of nineteenth-century positivism reveals valuable insights into that historical context and the complexities of its intellectual debates, as well as the critical contributions of such figures as Harriet Martineau.

168

Harriet Martineau's life was remarkably congruent with her beliefs and values as she determined her priorities, and lifestyle, and the employment of her energies and abilities. As a woman entirely dedicated to her vocation, she was consistent and persevering in her life conduct. Her intellectual pursuits centered on a quest for answers to philosophical questions and solutions to social and economic problems. In her "mission" as a public educator, she expressed her views with utter candor. She was committed to the idea of progress as the key to understanding history and to the improvement of society, her fundamental concern. Although tenacious in her viewpoints, formed quickly and sometimes prematurely, she had an exploring spirit and welcomed new ideas and experiences readily, particularly when her health and energies allowed. Like most thinkers, she did change her mind on a number of issues over the years (labor legislation, population control, for example); she continued to be, even at an age when she might have been excused, concerned about the problems and oppressions of others.

Martineau surely could feel, at the end of her busy and useful life, that she had lived it as she wished and had fulfilled the commitment of her youth to serve society and to educate its members to the best of her capabilities. At least twice before she had felt that death was not far off and, in 1855, chided herself for her obsession with death.

> I have now had three months' experience of the fact of constant expectation of death; and the result is, as much regret as a rational person can admit at the absurd waste of time, thought, and energy that I have been guilty of in the course of my life in dwelling on the subject of death ... I have tried to conceive, with the help of the sensations of my sinking-fits, the act of dying, and its attendant feelings; and thus far I have always gone to sleep in the middle of it ... I find death in prospect the simplest thing in the world – a thing not to be feared or regretted, or to get excited about in any way (*Auto.*, 2:435).

Her reflections of that period, when she truly was convinced that the end was near, remained consistent with her life and her summation of it. In consideration of her "last view of the world" (1855), Martineau contemplates the fate of the human race:

It is my deliberate opinion that the one essential requisite of human welfare in all ways is scientific knowledge of human nature. It is my belief that we can in no way but by sound knowledge of Man learn, fully and truly, any thing else; and that it is only when glimpses of that knowledge were opened, – however scantily and obscurely, – that men *have* effectually learned any thing else (*Auto.*, 2:458).

She remained convinced that the third stage in intellectual and social evolution, the Scientific stage, was at hand, and "the last of the mythologies is about to vanish before the flood of a brighter light." That bright light rested with "a true science of human nature." She felt that the new science would bring not only new knowledge and understanding, but also an enlarged capacity for human beings to create a just society and live heroic lives.

When our race is trained in the morality which belongs to ascertained truth, all 'fear and trembling' will be left to children; and men will have risen to a capacity for higher work than saving themselves, – to that of 'working out' the welfare of their race, not in 'fear and trembling', but with serene hope and joyful assurance.

The world as it is is growing somewhat dim before my eyes; but the world as it is to be looks brighter every day (*Auto.*, 2:461–62).

Notes

1. It is interesting to observe that men, including Mill and others, chose to bypass certain issues, for example birth control, as politically too threatening. In general, it was women like Harriet Martineau who analyzed the political and social issues which concerned the family and social welfare and which consequently affected women more dramatically than men. Their concerns resulted in critical analyses of patriarchy and male dominance, particularly in the family and in politics.
2. Martha S. Vogeler, *Frederic Harrison: The Vocations of a Positivist*, (Oxford: Clarendon Press, 1984), 253. It should be mentioned that Harrison had strong patriarchal attitudes ("woman as moral not material force") and undoubtedly saw Martineau as outside her proper sphere. He supported his wife's Anti-Suffrage League efforts, maintained that woman's place was in the home, and eschewed any attempts by women to attain goals outside the domestic sphere (See Frederic Harrison, *Realities and Ideals*, 1908).

Chronology

1802   12 June – Harriet Martineau born in Norwich, Norfolk, in Gurney House on Magdalen Street

1805   James Martineau born

1813   Harriet and sister Rachel attend Mr. Perry's school in Norwich

1814   Harriet's deafness ensues

1818   Harriet sent to Bristol to Aunt Kentish for schooling for one-and-a-half years. Lant Carpenter, her teacher, becomes major influence; daughter Mary Carpenter, her friend

1820   Ear trumpet needed

1822   First articles published in the *Monthy Repository*: "Female Writers of Practical Divinity" and "On Female Education"

1823   Harriet meets John Worthington, college friend of James

1824   Harriet's eldest brother Thomas dies

1824   Economic crash threatens Thomas Martineau's textile business

1826   June – Death of Harriet's father, Thomas Martineau
August – Worthington proposes to Harriet, who distresses herself by accepting. By December Worthington is ill and goes mad. Harriet asks for return for her letters and refuses to visit her fiancé

1827   May – Worthington dies. Harriet publishes first stories on political economy, *The Rioters* and *Principle and Practice*

1828   Harriet offers Fox assistance and regular contributions to the *Monthly Repository*

1829   Martineau family business collapses, leaving the Martineau women to support themselves. Harriet requests remuneration for *Monthly Repository* articles; Fox pays her £15 per year

1830   *Traditions of Palestine*. Harriet meets Gustav D'Eichtal and is introduced to the writings of Saint-Simon, French utopian socialist

171

1831	Prizes for her three essays on Unitarianism. Trip to Dublin to visit James with the £31. Begins political economy tales while staying with cousin Richard in London
1832 –34	Publishes 25 *Illustrations of Political Economy* First volume sells over 5,000 copies; series averaged 10,000 per month. Develops friendship with Malthus
1832	Moves to Fludyer Street, London, with mother and widowed aunt
1834	Publishes *Illustrations of Taxation* and *Poor Laws and Paupers*
1834	Travels to America
1836	Returns to England
1837	Publishes *Society in America*. Begins to keep a diary. Offered editorship of an economics periodical. First article in *London Westminster Review*
1838	Publishes *Retrospect of Western Travel* and *How To Observe Morals and Manners*. "The Martyr Age of the United States" in the *Westminster Review*. Journey to Scotland. Journey to the Continent; ill in Venice; brought home by her brothers
1839	*Guide to Service* and *Deerbrook* published
1839 –44	Ill at Tynemouth
1841	Publishes *The Hour and the Man* and the *Playfellow* Series.
1844	Recovers from illness by using mesmerism. Publishes *Life in the Sickroom*
1845	Publishes "Letters on Mesmerism" in the *Athenaeum* and *Dawn Island*, an anti-Corn Law tale. Meets Henry George Atkinson. Purchases lot in Ambleside, plans and builds her home, The Knoll
1845 –46	Publishes *Forest and Game Law Tales*
1846	April – Moves into The Knoll. Begins eight-month trip to the Middle East with the Yateses and Joseph Ewart
1847	Martineau renews friendship with Atkinson. Their exchange of letters begins
1848	Publishes *Eastern Life, Past and Present*. Begins her lectures in Ambleside which continue for several winters. Death of her mother at age 76

Select Bibliography

Works By Martineau

Addresses; with prayers and original hymns, for the use of families and schools, By a Lady. London: Rowland Hunter, 1826.

The Billow and The Rock: A Tale. London: Charles Knight, 1846.

Biographical Sketches. New York: Leypoldt & Holt, 1869, London: Macmillan, 1877.

British Rule in India: A Historical Sketch. London: Smith, Elder, 1857.

"Chicago in 1836. 'Strange Early Days,' by Harriet Martineau." *The Present and Future Prospects of Chicago*. Edited by H. Brown. Chicago: Fergus Printing, 1876.

Christmas Day, or, The Friends. London: Houlston, 1834.

A Complete Guide to the English Lakes. Windermere: John Garnett, 1855.

Dawn Island, A Tale. Manchester: J. Gadsby, 1845.

Deerbrook, A Novel. 3 vols. London: Edward Moxon, 1839.

Devotional Exercises, consisting of reflection and prayers, for the use of young persons; to which is added A treatise on the Lord's Supper, By a Lady. London: Rowland Hunter, 1823.

Eastern Life: Present and Past. 3 vols. London: Edward Moxon, 1848.

Endowed Schools of Ireland. London: Smith, Elder, 1859.

England and Her Soldiers. London: Smith, Elder, 1859.

The Essential Faith of the Universal Church: Deduced from the Sacred Records. London: The Unitarian Association, 1831.

The Factory Controversy; A Warning Against Meddling Legislation. Manchester: National Association of Factory Occupiers, 1855.

The Faith as Unfolded by Many Prophets. London: The Unitarian Association, 1832.

Five Years of Youth; or, Sense and Sentiment. London: Harvey and Darton, 1831.

Forest and Game Tales. 3 vols. London: Edward Moxon, 1845–46.

The Friends: A Continuation of Christmas-Day. London: Houlston, 1831.

Guide to Keswick and its environs. Windermere: John Garnett, 1857.

The Guide to Service: The Housemaid. 1839. *The Lady's Maid*. 1838. *The Maid of all Work*. 1838. London: Charles Knight.

The Hampdens: An Historiette. London: Routledge, 1880.

Harriet Martineau's Autobiography, with Memorials by Maria Weston Chapman. 3 vols. London: Elder, 1877.

Health, Husbandry, and Handicraft. London: Bradbury and Evans, 1861.

The History of England During the Thirty Years' Peace 1816–1846. 2 vols. London: Charles Knight, 1849.

A History of the American Compromises. London: John Chapman, 1856.

Introduction to *The History of the Peace, from 1800 to 1815*. London: Charles Knight, 1851.

The Hour and the Man: An Historical Romance. 3 vols. London: Cassell, 1841.

Household Education. London: Edward Moxon, 1849.

How to Observe Morals and Manners. London: Charles Knight, 1838; New Brunswick, N.J.: Transaction Publishers, with an introduction by Michael R. Hill, 1989.

Illustrations of Political Economy. 9 vols. London: Charles Fox, 1832–34.

Illustrations of Taxation. 5 parts. London: Charles Fox, 1834.

Letters From Ireland. London: John Chapman, 1852.

Letters on Mesmerism. London: Edward Moxon, 1845.

Letters On The Laws of Man's Nature and Development, with Henry G. Atkinson. London: John Chapman, 1851; Boston: Josiah Mendum, 1889.

Life in the Sickroom: Essays by an Invalid. London: Edward Moxon, 1844.

The "Manifest Destiny" of the American Union. New York: American Anti-Slavery Society, 1857.

The Martyr Age of the United States. New York: S.W. Benedict, 1839.

Introduction to *Mind Amongst the Spindles, The Lowell Offering: A Miscellany Wholly Composed by the Factory Girls of an American City*. London: Charles Knight, 1844.

Miscellanies. 2 vols. Boston: Hilliard Grey, 1836.

My Servant Rachel: A Tale. London: Houlston, 1838.

Our Farm of Two Acres. New York: Bunce and Huntington, 1865.

The Playfellow: Settlers At Home. The Peasant and the Prince. Feats on the Fjord. The Crofton Boys. 4 vols. London: Charles Knight, 1841.

Poor Laws and Paupers Illustrated. 4 parts. London: Charles Fox, 1833.

The Positive Philosophy of Auguste Comte, freely translated and condensed by Harriet Martineau. 2 vols. London: John Chapman, 1853.

Principle and Practice; or the Orphan Family. Wellington: Houlston, 1827.

Providence as manifested through Israel: An Essay . . . Issued by the British and Foreign Unitarian Association and addressed to the Jews. London: The Unitarian Association, 1831.

Retrospect of Western Travel. 3 vols. London: Saunders and Otley, 1838.

The Rioters, or, a Tale of Bad Times. Wellington: Houlston, 1827.

Sequel to Principle and Practice; or, The Orphan Family. London: Houlston, 1831.

Introduction to Reinhold Pauli's *Simon de Montfort, Earl of Leicester, The Creator of the House of Commons*. Translated by Una M. Goodwin. London: Trubner & Co., 1876.

Sketches From Life. London: Whittaker; Windermere: J. Garnett 1856.

Society in America. 3 vols. London: Saunders and Otley, 1837; Condensed edition, with an introduction by Seymour Martin Lipset. Garden City: Doubleday Anchor, 1962.

Suggestions Towards the Future Government of India. London: Smith, Elder, 1858.

The tendency of strikes and sticks to produce low wages, and of union between masters and men to ensure good wages. Durham: J.H. Veitch, 1834.

Traditions of Palestine. London: Longman, Rees, Orme Brown and Greene, 1830.

The Turn-out; or Patience the Best Policy. Wellington: Houlston, 1829.

Martineau published in numerous periodicals and newspapers.

Articles cited include:

"Domestic Service." *London and Westminster Review* 29 (August 1838): 405–32.

"The Martyr Age of the United States." *The London and Westminster Review* 32 (December 1838): 1–59.

"Letter from Miss Martineau," *Mind amongst the Spindles: A Selection from the Lowell Offering*, Charles Knight, ed. (London: C. Knight, 1844): xvii–xxii.

"New Schools for Wives." *Household Words* 5 (April 10, 1852): 84–89.

"England's Foreign Policy," *Westminster Review* 61 (January 1854): 190–232.

"Results of the Census of 1851." *Westminster Review* 61 (April 1854): 323–57.

"'Manifest Destiny' of the American Union." *Westminster Review* 68 (July 1857): 1–25.

"Female Dress in 1857." *Westminster Review* 68 (October 1857): 315–40.

"The Slave-trade in 1858." *Edinburgh Review* 108 (October 1858): 276–99.

"Female Industry." *Edinburgh Review* 109 (April 1859): 151–73.

"Miss Nightingale's Notes on Nursing." *Quarterly Review* 107 (April 1860): 392–422.

"Modern Domestic Service." *Edinburgh Review* 115 (April 1862): 409–39.

"Convict System in England and Ireland." *Edinburgh Review* 117 (January 1863): 241–68.

"Cooperative Societies in 1864." *Edinburgh Review* 120 (October 1864): 407–36

"Middle-Class Education in England: Boys." *Cornhill Magazine* 10 (October 1864): 409–26.

"Middle-Class Education in England: Girls." *Cornhill Magazine* 10 (November 1864): 549–68.

"Nurses Wanted." *Cornhill Magazine* 11 (April 1865): 409–25.

"Life in the Criminal Class." *Edinburgh Review* 122 (October 1865): 337–71.

"Salem Witchcraft." *Edinburgh Review* 128 (July 1868): 1–47.

Collections of Letters

Arbuckle, Elisabeth Sanders, ed. *Harriet Martineau's Letters to Fanny Wedgwood*. Stanford, California: Stanford University Press, 1983.

Sanders, Valerie, ed. *Harriet Martineau: Selected Letters*. Oxford: Clarendon Press, 1990.

Secondary Sources

Altick, Richard D. *The English Common Reader: A Social History of Mass Reading Public 1800–1900*. Chicago: University of Chicago Press, 1957.

Annan, Noel. *The Curious Strength of Positivism in English Political Thought*. London: Oxford University Press, 1959.

Banks, Olive. *Becoming a Feminist: The Social Origins of 'First Wave' Feminism*. Brighton: Harvester Press, 1986.

———, *Faces of Feminism: A Study of Feminism as a Social Movement*. Oxford: Martin Robertson, 1981.

Benn, Alfred William. *The History of English Rationalism in the Nineteenth Century*. 2 vols. New York: Russell and Russell, 1962.

Blaug, Mark. "The Myth of the Old Poor Law and the Making of the New." *The Journal of Economic History* 22 (1963): 151–84.

———, "Political Economy to Be Read as Literature." Chap. 7 in *Ricardian Economics: A Historical Study*. New Haven: Yale University Press, 1958.

———, "The Poor Law Report Reexamined." *Journal of Economic History* 24 (1964): 229–45.

Bosanquet, Theodora. *Harriet Martineau: An Essay in Comprehension*. London: Etchels and Macdonald, 1927.

Burrow, John W. *Evolution and Society: A Study in Victorian Social Theory*. Cambridge: Cambridge University Press, 1966.

Cannon, Walter F. "The Normative Role of Science in Early Victorian Thought." *Journal of The History of Ideas* 25 (1964): 487–502.

Cazamian, Louis. *The Social Novel in England 1830–1850*. Translated by Martin Fido. London: Routledge and Paul, 1973.

Colby, Vineta. "Domestic Devotion and Hearthside Heroism: Harriet Martineau's *Deerbrook* and the Novel of Community." *Yesterday's Woman: Domestic Realism in the English Novel*. Princeton: Princeton University Press, 1974.

Collins, Philip. Introduction to *Hard Times*, by Charles Dickens. London: Dent, Everyman's Library, 1978.

Colson, Percy. "Virtue Is Its Own Reward [Harriet Martineau]." *Victorian Portraits*. Freeport, New York: Books For Libraries Press, 1932; reprinted 1968.

Courtney, Jane E. *The Adventurous Thirties: A Chapter in the Woman's Movement*. London: Oxford University Press, 1933.

———, "Harriet Martineau." *Freethinkers of the Nineteenth Century*. London: Chapman and Hall, 1920.

Cruse, Amy. *The Victorians and Their Books*. London: George Allen and Unwin, 1935.

David, Deirdre. *Intellectual Women and Victorian Patriarchy: Harriet Martineau, Elizabeth Barrett Browning, George Eliot*. Ithaca, New York: Cornell University Press, 1987.

Dentith, Simon. "Political Economy, Fiction and The Language of Practical Ideology in Nineteenth-Century England." *Social History* 8 (1983): 183–99.

Drummond, James and C.B. Upton. *The Life and Letters of James Martineau*. 2 vols. London: James Nisbet, 1902.

Eliot, George. *The British Quarterly Review* xi (1850): 355–71.

Farmer, M.E. "The Positivist Movement and the Development of English Sociology." *Sociological Review* 15 (1967): 5–20.

Fay, C.R. "Economics in a Novel." *Dalhousie Review* 12 (1932): 180–81.

Fielding, K.J. and Anne Smith. "*Hard Times* and the Factory Controversy: Dickens vs. Harriet Martineau." *Nineteenth Century Fiction* 24 (1970): 404–27.

Fraser, Rebecca. *The Brontës: Charlotte Brontë and Her Family*. New York: Fawcett Columbine, 1988.

Froude, James Anthony. "Materialism: Miss Martineau and Mr. Atkinson." *Fraser's* 43 (1851): 418–34.

Garnett, Richard. *The Life of W.J. Fox*. London: John Lane, The Bodley Head, 1910.

Gaskell, E.C. *The Life of Charlotte Brontë*. (1857) Reprint. London: J.M. Dent, 1908.

Greenhow, Thomas M. *Medical Report of the Case of Miss-H-M*. 1845.

———, "Termination of the Case of Miss Harriet Martineau." *British Medical Journal*, 850 (1877): 449–50.

Greg, W.R. "Harriet Martineau." *Nineteenth Century* 2 (1877). Reprinted in *Miscellaneous Essays*. London: Trubner & Co., (1882): 176–205.

Grylls, R. Glynn. "Emancipation of Women." *Ideas and Beliefs of the Victorians: An Historic Revaluation of the Victorian Age*. New York: E.P. Dutton, 1966: 254–60.

Haight, Gordon S., ed. *The George Eliot Letters*. 6 Vols. New Haven: Yale University Press, 1954.

Harrison, Frederic. "Harriet Martineau's Positive Philosophy." *Positivist Review* 4 (1896): 92–98.

Hayden, Dolores. *The Grand Domestic Revolution*. Cambridge, Mass.: The MIT Press, 1981.

Himmelfarb, Gertrude. *The Idea of Poverty: England in the Early Industrial Age*. New York: Random House, 1983.

Hoecker, James J. *Joseph Priestley and the Idea of Progress*. New York: Garland Publishing Inc., 1987.

Hoecker-Drysdale, Susan. "The Vocation of Harriet Martineau: A Victorian Vision of Science and Society," unpublished paper presented at Trinity College, Dublin, 1987.

Holcombe, Lee. *Victorian Ladies at Work: Middle-Class Working Women in England and Wales, 1850–1914*. Hamden, Connecticut: Archon Books, 1973.

————, *Wives and Property: Reform of the Married Women's Property Law in Nineteenth-Century England*. Toronto: University of Toronto, 1983.

Holt, Raymond V. *The Unitarian Contribution to Social Progress in England*. London: Lindsay Press, 1938.

Holyoake, George L. "Harriet Martineau." *The National Reformer* (July 9, 1876): 17–18.

Horne, Richard H. "Harriet Martineau and Mrs. Jameson." *A New Spirit of the Age*. London: Oxford University Press, 1907.

Houghton, Walter E. *The Victorian Frame of Mind, 1830–70*. New Haven: Yale University Press, 1957.

Kamm, Josephine. *Rapiers and Battleaxes: The Women's Movement and its Aftermath*. London: George Allen & Unwin, 1966.

Kaplan, F. "Mesmeric Mania: The Early Victorians and Animal Magnetism." *Journal of the History of Ideas* 35 (1974): 691–702.

Kestner, Joseph. *Protest and Reform: The British Social Narrative by Women, 1827–1867*. London: Methuen, 1985.

Lohrli, Anne, compiler. *Household Words: A Weekly Journal 1850–59 Conducted by Charles Dickens*. Toronto: University of Toronto Press, 1973.

Longford, Elizabeth. *Eminent Victorian Women*. London: Weidenfeld and Nicolson, 1981.

Marks, Patricia. "Harriet Martineau: *Fraser*'s Maid of [Dis]Honour." *Victorian Periodicals Review* XIX (1986): 28–34.

Martin, Robert B. "Charlotte Brontë and Harriet Martineau." *Nineteenth-Century Fiction* 7 (1952): 198–201.

Martineau, David. *Pedigrees of the Martineau Family*. 1907. Revised edition by C. Anthony Crofton, printed for private circulation, 1972.

Martineau, James "Mesmeric Atheism." *Prospective Review*, 7 (1851): 224–62.

Marvin, F.S. "Harriet Martineau: Triumph and Tragedy." *Hibbert Journal* 25 (1926): 631–40.

Marx, Karl. *Economic and Philosophic Manuscripts of 1844*. Moscow: Foreign Languages Publishing House, 1961.

McCrone, Kathleen. "The National Association for the Promotion of Social Science and the Advancement of Victorian Women." *Atlantis* 8 (1982): 44–66.

Meynell, Alice. "A Woman of Masculine Understanding." *The Wares of Autolycus: Selected Literary Essays of Alice Meynell.* Introduced by P.M. Fraser. London: Oxford University Press, 1965.

Miller, F. Fenwick. *Harriet Martineau.* London: W.H. Allen, 1884.

Murray, Robert H. *Studies in the English Social and Political Thinkers of the Nineteenth Century.* 2 vols. Cambridge: W. Heffer and Sons, 1929.

Myers, Mitzi. "Harriet Martineau's *Autobiography*: the Making of a Female Philosopher" *Women's Autobiography: Essays in Criticism.* Edited by Estelle Jelinek. Bloomington: Indiana University Press, 1980a: 53–70.

———, "Unmothered Daughter and Radical Reformer: Harriet Martineau's Career." *The Lost Tradition: Mothers and Daughters in Literature.* Edited by Cathy Davidson and E.M. Broner. New York: Frederick Ungar, 1980b: 70–80.

Nevill, John Cranstoun. *Harriet Martineau.* London: Frederick Muller, 1943.

Nicholson, Norman, comp. *The Lake District: An Anthology.* Harmondsworth: Penguin Books, 1977.

———, *The Lakers: The Adventures of the First Tourists.* London: Robert Hale, 1955.

O'Donnell, Margaret G. "Harriet Martineau: A Popular Early Economics Educator." *The Journal of Economic Education* (Fall 1983): 59–64.

Parssinen, T.M. "Popular Science and Society: the Phrenological Movement in Early Victorian Britain." *Journal of Social History* 8 (1974): 1–20.

Parton, James. "Harriet Martineau." *Daughters of Genius: A Series of Sketches.* Philadelphia: Hubbard Brothers, 1888.

Payn, James. *Some Literary Recollections.* London: Smith, Elder, 1884.

Peterson, Linda H. "Martineau's *Autobiography*: The Feminine Debate over Self-Interpretation." *Victorian Autobiography: The Tradition of Self-Interpretation.* New Haven: Yale University Press, 1986.

Pichanick, Valerie Kossew. *Harriet Martineau: The Woman and Her Work, 1802–76.* Ann Arbor: The University of Michigan Press, 1980.

Polanyi, Karl. *The Great Transformation: The Political and Economic Origins of Our Time.* Boston: Beacon Press, 1944.

Poovey, Mary. *Uneven Developments: The Ideological Work of Gender in Mid-Victorian England.* Chicago: The University of Chicago Press, 1988.

Pope-Hennessey, Una. "Harriet Martineau." *Three English Women in America.* London: Benn, 1929.

Postlethwaite, Diana. *Making It Whole: A Victorian Circle and the Shape of Their World.* Columbus: Ohio University Press, 1984.

———, "Mothering and Mesmerism in the Life of Harriet Martineau." *Signs: Journal of Women in Culture and Society* 14 (1989): 583–609.

Rendall, Jane. *The Origins of Modern Feminism: Women in Britain, France and the United States, 1780–1860*. New York: Schocken Books, 1984.

Richardson, Henry. "Harriet Martineau's Account of Herself." *The Contemporary Review* 24 (1877): 1114–15.

Rivenburg, Narola Elizabeth. "Harriet Martineau: An Example of Victorian Conflict," Ph.D. diss., Columbia University, 1932.

Rivlin, Joseph B. *Harriet Martineau: A Bibliography of Her Separately Printed Books*. New York: The New York Public Library, 1947.

Rose, Phyllis, *Parallel Lives: Five Victorian Marriages*. New York: Random House, 1984.

Rossi, Alice S. "The First Woman Sociologist: Harriet Martineau." *The Feminist Papers: From Adams to de Beauvoir*. Edited by Alice S. Rossi. New York: Columbia University Press, 1973; Bantam Books, 1974: 118–43.

Sanders, Valerie. *Reason Over Passion: Harriet Martineau and the Victorian Novel*. Sussex: Harvester Press, 1986.

Sanderson, Michael. *Education, Economic Change and Society in England, 1780–1870*. London: Macmillan Press, 1983.

Seat, William R., Jr. "Harriet Martineau in America." *Notes and Queries* 204 (1959): 207–8.

Simon, Walter M. "Auguste Comte's English Disciples." *Victorian Studies* 8 (1964–65): 161–72.

———, *European Positivism in the Nineteenth-Century: An Essay in Intellectual History*. New York: 1963.

Smith, Sidonie. "Harriet Martineau's *Autobiography*." *A Poetics of Women's Autobiography: Marginality and the Fictions of Self-Representation*. Bloomington: Indiana University Press, 1987.

Smith-Rosenberg, Carroll. *Disorderly Conduct: Visions of Gender in Victorian America*. New York: Oxford University Press, 1985.

Spender, Dale. "Harriet Martineau." *Women of Ideas and What Men Have Done To Them, From Aphra Behn to Adrienne Rich*. London: Routledge and Kegan Paul, 1982: 125–35.

Stephen, Leslie. "Martineau, Harriet." *Dictionary of National Biography* 12:1194–99. Oxford: University Press, 1917.

Taylor, Barbara. *Eve and The New Jerusalem: Socialism and Feminism in the Nineteenth-Century*. London: Virago Press, 1983.

Taylor, Clare. *British and American Abolitionists: An Episode in Trans-Atlantic Understanding*. Edinburgh: Edinburgh University Press, 1974.

Terry, James L. "Bringing Women . . . In: A Modest Proposal." *Teaching Sociology* 10 (1983): 251–61.

Thomas, Gillian. *Harriet Martineau*. Boston: Twayne Publishers, 1985.

Thomson, Dorothy L. "Harriet Martineau." *Adam Smith's Daughters*. Hicksville, N.Y.: Exposition, 1973.

Tillotson, Geoffrey and Kathleen. *Mid-Victorian Studies*. London: The Athlone Press, University of London, 1965.

Tillotson, Kathleen. *The Novels of the Eighteen Forties*. Oxford: Clarendon Press, 1954.

Vincent, David. *Bread, Knowledge and Freedom: A Study of Nineteenth-Century Working Class Autobiography*. London: Europa Publications, 1981.

Vogeler, Martha S. *Frederic Harrison: The Vocations of a Positivist*. Oxford: Clarendon Press, 1984.

Walters, Margaret. "Mary Wollstonecraft, Harriet Martineau and Simone de Beauvoir." *The Rights and Wrongs of Women*. Edited by Juliet Mitchell and Ann Oakley. Harmondsworth: Penguin, 1976: 304–78.

Watts, Ruth E. "The Unitarian Contribution to the Development of Female Education (1790–1850)." *History of Education* 9 (1980): 273–86.

Webb, Robert K. *The British Working Class Reader 1790–1848*. London: George Allen and Unwin, 1955.

———, *A Handlist of Contributions to the Daily News by Harriet Martineau, 1852–1866*. 1959.

———, *Harriet Martineau: A Radical Victorian*. New York: Columbia University Press, 1960.

———, *Modern England From the Eighteenth Century to the Present*. New York: Dodd, Mead, 1970.

Weiner, Gaby. "Harriet Martineau: A Reassessment." *Feminist Theorists: Three Centuries of Key Women Thinkers*. Edited by Dale Spender. New York: Pantheon Books, 1983.

Wheatley, Vera. *The Life and Work of Harriet Martineau*. London: Secker and Warburg, 1957.

Wolff, Robert L. "Harriet Martineau's Novel, *Ireland*." *Ireland: From The Act of Union (1800) to the Death of Parnell (1891)*. New York: Garland Press, 1979.

Woodham-Smith, Cecil. *Florence Nightingale, 1820–1910*. London: Constable and Co., 1950.

Wright, T.R. *The Religion of Humanity: The Impact of Comtean Positivism on Victorian Britain*. Cambridge: Cambridge University, 1986.

Yates, Gayle Graham, ed. *Harriet Martineau on Women*. New Brunswick, New Jersey: Rutgers University Press, 1985.

Index

Lovejoy, E. P., 68

Madison, James, 53, 76 n.5
Malthus, Thomas, 14, 26, 35, 38, 40, 166
Manchester College, 13
Marcet, Jane, 31, 137–38, 165
Martineau, Ellen (Higginson), 17 n.1, n.2
Martineau, Elizabeth (Greenhow), 16 n.1, 79
Martineau, Elizabeth Rankin, 7, 8, 17 n.2, 138
Martineau, Gaston, 7
Martineau, Henry, 17 n.1
Martineau, James, 13, 17 n.1, n.3, 21, 32, 34, 71, 81, 84, 89–90, 92 n.14, 111, 138, 164
Martineau, Rachel, 17 n.1
Martineau, Richard (cousin), 32
Martineau, Robert, 17 n.1
Martineau, Thomas Sr., 7, 8, 24
Martineau, Thomas Jr., 13, 16 n.1, 24
Martineau, Maria (niece), 147
Martineau family: financial disaster, 29–30
Martineau, Harriet:
  adolescence, 12–14
  agnosticism, 84, 85, 87, 89, 90, 111
  authorship, 21, 34, 35
  her autobiography, 138–40
  on biography and history, 137–38
  character and personality, 3, 54, 153, 160, 161–62, 163
  childhood, 7–16, 17 n.4, 90 n.2
  deafness, 9, 12, 17 n.4, 21, 24, 30, 105
  death, 156
  editorship opportunities, 70–71, 160
  engagement, 24
  family, 8–12, 17, 82–83
  farming, 93–95
  ideas on childbearing. *See* children and socialization
  intellect, 169
  intellectual influences on, 12, 14–15, 21, 26–27
  invalidism, 79–80; recovery, 82
  the Knoll, 93–95
  lectures, 107, 124 n.4, 110
  languages, 11–13, 30, 101
  model of society, 27, 44, 52
  others' views of Martineau, 87–88,

159–64
  physical problems and illnesses, 9, 24, 78–79, 81–84, 90 n.2, 142–43, 148
  popularity of Martineau and her writings, 33–34, 45, 46, 69, 70, 74, 80, 95, 107, 114, 133, 153, 160, 165, 168
  positivism, 15–16, 91 n.7, 110, 111, 164
  pseudonyms, 22
  public education, 32, 35
  and publishers, 32–33, 50, 69, 107, 110, 139
  readership, 21
  reading and education, 10–12, 13
  refusal of government pension, 129–30, 155 n.2
  relationship with brother James, 13, 89–90, 164
  relationship with mother, 8–10, 12, 30–31, 83, 138
  religion, 8, 11, 14, 16, 26, 88, 89, 99, 101–4, 161
  religious writings, 14, 25
  self-image, 9, 158–59
  requests from other countries, 160
  travels, 75–76 n.3, 78, 95–101, 104
  self-obituary, 158–59
  views on education, 134
  views on death, 156, 169–70
  views on marriage, 24–25, 40; sexual orientation, 91 n.6
  views on prisons and punisment, 132
  views on science and philosophy, 28, 83, 84–85, 88–89, 151–53
  views on unions, 40–42, 132, 134
  work in journalism, 133–37
  writing habits, 34–35, 110
Martineau's Writings:
  Addresses; with prayers and original hymns (1826), 14
  Autobiography (1855), 16
  The Billow and The Rock (1846), 95
  Biographical Sketches (1869), 137–38, 141 n.6
  British Rule in India (1857), 122, 126 n.17
  Dawn Island, a Tale (1845), 95
  Demerara (1832), 38–39, 65–66
  "Domestic Service in England" (1838), 117–18
  Deerbrook (1838), 72–74, 90 n.1,

190